A Saint in Glory Stands

A Saint
in Glory
Stands

The story of Alva J. McClain,
Founder of Grace Theological Seminary

Norman B. Rohrer

BMH Books
P.O. Box 544
Winona Lake, Indiana 46590

Acknowledgments

I am grateful to Dr. Homer A. Kent, Jr., president of Grace Schools, for initiating this editorial project, to Rev. Charles W. Turner for seeing to its manufacture, and to Mrs. McClain and her husband's two surviving sisters -- Mary Ellen Miller and Ruth Ashman -- for their help in recalling Godsends throughout Alva J. McClain's eight decades. The 1951 Yearbook *Xapis*, in which Dr. McClain wrote "The Background and Origin of Grace Theological Seminary," and the book, *Conquering Frontiers, a history of the Brethren Church* (BMH Books, 1972) by the late Homer A. Kent, Sr., have provided valuable reference material.

Copyright 1986
BMH Books
Winona Lake, Indiana

ISBN: 0-88469-183-7

Printed in USA

Cover design by Mike Boze

In appreciation
of your years of faithful support to
Grace College & Theological Seminary

Mrs. Alva J. McClain

Herman A. Hoyt, Th.D.

Homer A. Kent, Jr., Th.D.

John J. Davis, Th.D.

To those who heard him preach
and followed his Lord

Table of Contents

Preface

Any theologian who may hope (or fear) that someone may write the story of his life should pray that he not fall into the hands of an enemy, a disciple, a rival, or a relative, the late A. W. Tozer once pointed out.

These types, he thought, make the poorest biographers. Their relationship puts them where they are unable to view the subject as he really is, so the portrait that emerges, however interesting, is never true to the original.

I come to the chronicling of Alva J. McClain's life as from a far country, free from the handicap of any of the precarious relationships mentioned above, although bringing to the project a sympathetic heart and an objective mind.

Those of us who knew him are richer because he lived and wrote and preached and taught. Blessed with such benefits, we are forever bound to thank our loving Lord for giving him to the Church.

The weight and power of his teachings, the beauty of his quiet and reverent spirit, his exemplary marriage, and his patience when others disagreed with him -- all this presses in upon us and we, like Daniel, "sit down astonied."

The founder of Grace Theological Seminary was obedient to every call from his Lord: He came to Him and found rest . . . he followed Him and became an ally in the work of Christ and His Kingdom . . . and he abided in Him to glorify God and enjoy a victorious Christian walk.

From the first to the last of Alva J. McClain's 80 years I have praised him most by painting him truest.

--Norman B. Rohrer

1

*'Well, of course, **I** believe . . . '*

Excerpts from classroom, pulpit and writings

ON THE BIBLE

The Bible is one book. Had we to give that book a title, we might with justice call it "The Book of the Coming Kingdom of God." That is, indeed its central theme everywhere. In approving this affirmation we are not forgetting the person and work of our Lord Jesus Christ. For *He* is the King eternal, and there could be no final kingdom apart from Him and His work as the Lamb slain from the foundation of the world.

ON INSPIRATION

You have watched the skillful musician place his fingers upon the keyboard of the organ. And then you have heard the whispering of the winds, the crash and thunder of the storm, the tramp of armies, the chiming of the bells, and perhaps the sobbing as of a heart torn with grief. Is the eternal God less a genius than man? To sound forth his revelation he used a human keyboard extending over sixty centuries. When he chose to reveal the coming of the only begotten Son into the world, he laid his right hand upon Enoch, the seventh from Adam, and his left hand upon John, the weary exile of Patmos. The celestial hymn began with Enoch, "Behold, the Lord cometh with ten thousand of his saints." And in the eternal harmony of revelation, the voice of John echoes in response, "Behold, he cometh with clouds, and every eye shall see him!"

ON THE DEITY OF CHRIST

As to His humanity, He was *made* of the seed of David, but as to His deity, He was *declared.* Humanity is a created thing but deity is uncreated. The human nature, or flesh of Christ, was made at a definite point in human history, but His divine nature was existing from eternity and needed only to be declared that men might see it.

ON LOVE

Some have said that the mark of a true disciple is love, not doctrine. I submit to you that it is both love *and* doctrine. In Galatians one, verse eight, the Apostle Paul warns that "if any preach any other gospel unto you than that which we have preached unto you, let him be accursed." In the Apostle Paul's epistle to the Philippians he rejoices that the gospel is preached even by people who are doing it to spite him. I submit to you that the mark of a true disciple is love *and* doctrine.

ON JUSTIFICATION

After a man is justified, he discovers that he has a sin nature which gives rise to sinful acts. What will God do about that? The answer is sanctification, and that aspect of the work of God which deals with the power and pollution of sin. In sanctification, God deals with something that is actual, the power of sin. Whereas justification deals with the *guilt* of sin, sanctification deals with the *power of sin.*

ON PERSEVERANCE

Will this divine method of justification and sanctification last? The eighth chapter of Romans was written to answer that question, and the whole burden of the chapter is this: if you are in Christ Jesus, you are safe! Justification and sanctification in Christ will endure.

ON RIGHTEOUSNESS

God's righteousness is something not only that we *believe* but also something to which we should be *submitted.* One of the primary reasons why more men do not believe the simple gospel of God is because of human pride and human reason. They are determined not to *submit.* It is hard for all of us to submit and yield. The central issue is just submitting ourselves. That is all we need to do with this righteousness. Just let God put it on you.

ON CHRISTIAN SERVICE

We believers are the *douloi* of the Lord -- the bond servants. That term ought to be precious to us; it not only expresses the idea of our servitude to Christ, but reminds us that our servitude is based on purchase. I am a bondslave of the Lord because He bought me with His own precious blood. If you remember that, you will love to be called a servant of the Lord. I am not only obliged to serve Him, but I am His possession! He is responsible for me -- to take care of me and provide for me.

ON OVERSIMPLIFICATION

In the field of Christian theology . . . oversimplification may cause men to miss the richness and infinite variety of Christian truth in the interest of a barren unity. It was William James who once suggested that, considered from a certain abstract standpoint, even a masterpiece of violin music might be described as "a scraping of horses' tails over cats' bowels!" Such a definition, of course, has the great merit of simplicity; it gets rid of all the mystery of personality and the nuances of human genius. But the residue is not very interesting.

ON SCHOLARSHIP

It is wrong to say that fundamentalists are not interested in scholarship. They are interested, but they are busy with other things -- founding churches, preaching the gospel . . . . Sometimes it's difficult to hold men in college who are on fire to preach. They want to be out winning men to Christ. Somebody's going to have to do the scholarship. We need the best brains we've got on the mission field and in our churches. Despite the urgency of the hour, you ought to take time to prepare yourself.

ON PROPHECY

Viewed from one standpoint, prophecy arises out of a definite historical situation existing immediately before the eyes of the prophet. There is probably no exception to this rule. No matter how far into the future he was transported in vision, the prophet never lost his contact with history. He never forgot *where* he was, nor the people to whom he was sent to speak on behalf of God. Even in purely predictive prophecy, or what some have called apocalyptic vision, although the prophet may say little or nothing about the immediate historical situation, it is nevertheless not forgotten but furnishes the background of all that he has to say with reference to the future.

ON THE MILLENNIUM

The mediatorial reign of *Christ* is not limited to this precise measure of time. The record specifically states that this measure applies to the reign of the *saints:*

"they . . . shall reign with him a thousand years" (Revelation 20:6). In a very real sense, the mediatorial reign of Christ Himself may be said to begin *de jure* with His judicial work from heaven, as suggested by the announcement in 11:16 -- "The kingdoms of this world are become the kingdoms of our Lord, and of his Christ." And not only so, but His mediatorial reign extends beyond the end of the thousand years. "For he must reign," Paul writes, "till he hath put all enemies under his feet." The last enemy that shall be destroyed is death" (I Corinthians 15:25-26). And the destruction of death is beyond the end of the thousand years (Revelation 20:7,14).

ON WAR

Warfare is nothing unusual among the nations of the earth. The seasons of peace, in the recorded history of the world, have been very few and disconcertingly brief . . . . Considering the sinful nature of men, nothing else could be reasonably expected: "There is no peace, saith the Lord, unto the wicked" (Isaiah 48:22). This must be an axiom in a moral universe.

ON MESSIAH'S OFFER

The Lord did not grow discouraged over the apparent failure of His early ministry and set out deliberately to force the Jews to kill Him. The truth is that Jesus offered Himself as the Messianic King of Israel, that the offer was genuine, and therefore the nation *should* have accepted Him. To argue otherwise is to forget the demands of moral obligation and to set up a facade of forced theological unity which obscures the reality of the movements of history.

ON POPULARITY

There had been a time when, impressed by our Lord's supernatural power, [the Jews] had been ready to take Him by force and make Him king. But now they see Him, where He had never been before, apparently helpless in the hands of Roman authorities. Does anyone suppose that the astute and highly intelligent Jewish leaders would fail to exploit the situation to their own advantage with the crowd? How easy now to point out the appalling incongruity before the eyes -- the King of the Jews wearing a crown of thorns! Did the applause of the people, disappointed in their "hero," turn swiftly into vicious anger? If so, nothing could have been more plausible psychologically. History has shown more than once that the disappointment of the "people" can easily become a very terrible and violent thing.

ON GOVERNMENT

It is easy to forget that "we the people" in the long run must always pay for whatever the government does for us. Only fools suppose that by committing a matter to the government, they can get it done for nothing. Still worse, human government not only makes the people pay for everything done for them, but it always makes them pay more than it should cost. For only a part of the wealth taken by the government ever comes back to the people in services. No lesson in human history is taught more clearly than this, yet the lesson apparently is never learned.

ON CHILDREN

A child should never learn that it is possible to disobey his parents. If he does, you're surely licked, because his patience will always outlast yours.

ON DISCRIMINATION

Concerning the government's anti-discrimination stance which states that there shall be no discrimination on the basis of race, creed, color, or national origin, there's a hooker in there. I wonder if you see it. Surely we must not discriminate against a person because of his race or color, or national origin. But "creed" is in an entirely different category. A man does decide on his creed, and of course we have to discriminate in that regard. Do you mean I must accept an atheist to teach in our seminary?

ON TRANSPORTATION

The finest motor car built in America today is the Buick.

ON INDUSTRY

A man should know how to do something more than read a book.

ON CONDUCT IN THE NEW BUILDING

Pop shall be drunk only in the basement.

2

Preacher on the Pig Farm

Great leaders of the world usually enter incognito. Perhaps the rugged youngsters of Jesse would not have shoved their youngest brother around quite as roughly during their ancient equivalent of leap frog if they had known what the Lord had in mind for David later on. Perhaps the elders of The Brethren Church would have taken greater notice of that baby's first cry wafted across the sweet air of the Iowa countryside on April 11, 1888 had they known what part the newborn would play in affairs of their newly organized denomination. In that same year -- perhaps on the very day -- the trustees of the church's college wrote into their guidelines that "the training of Christian ministers would always be sacredly regarded as one of Ashland College's major functions." This lad, in the providence of God, would play a big part in carrying out that injunction.

Mary Ellen Gnagey McClain heard the cry of her baby that day and smiled. And when they announced that her second child was a boy she might have wept a little too there in the upstairs bedroom of the white clapboard farm house on the outskirts of Aurelia, Iowa.

The father, lay preacher and hog farmer Walter Scott McClain, was plowing black earth when neighbors summoned him urgently to the house. Mary, his chunky Pennsylvania Dutch wife, presented their second child to him as their two-year-old daughter Georgia Ada stood by the bed. Walter held him up and proclaimed proudly and prophetically to the gathered neighbors: "Here is our preacher." Even when his son earned a reputation as community prankster, practiced joker, and a young man bent on worldly pursuits, the farmer never lost that vision or charged God foolishly for unanswered prayer.

No one knows where farmer McClain got the name for his son. There is no record that anyone -- family or friend -- ever asked. Standing there before the family Bible, his broadcloth close-buttoned to the chin, Walter took his pen and wrote: "Alva Jay McClain." The discovery, as late as 1984, that Alva's middle name had been "Jay" all along instead of just the initial "J" came as a surprise to his two surviving sisters, Mary Miller and Ruth Ashman in Seal Beach, California. They, as did Alva himself, had always assumed that his middle name was simply the initial "J". As for the first name, well, Father McClain knew his Bible, and probably had remembered the dukes that came of Esau and liked especially the name of "duke Alvah" in Genesis 36:40.

As the neighbors gathered in to see the newest member of Aurelia they probably remarked with that special liberty friends allow themselves on such occasions, that the noble-sounding name was pretty hefty for such a wee one to carry, and if he lives a month with such a fine name he is as good as reared! Mary's face glows with joy and even the short, quiet farmer with the black hair and the piercing blue eyes allows himself a considered smile.

Walter had been ordained to the ministry of The Brethren Church only six years earlier by the reformer Henry Ritz Holsinger himself. The instigator of the denominational split in 1882 which divided the Old Orders from the German Baptists and spawned a new progressive assembly, was fiery and impatient. Walter, by contrast, was longsuffering with those who disagreed. That's not to say the farmer didn't have strong convictions. On the issue of wearing the black garb of the Taufers he told the old guard goodnaturedly, "I can't find in the Bible that you have to wear plain clothes." Aside, he confided to Mary that the old church was "so proud of its humility that all rewards were cancelled."

How this Scotsman had infiltrated the Dunkards of Masontown, Pennsylvania where Walter McClain was born is not known, but he was counted among the people of thrift and green thumbs whom William Penn himself had recruited from the fertile valleys of Germany to populate a Commonwealth granted him by the Crown of England.

Mary's progressive spirit matched that of her lay preacher husband. An attractive woman of few words, with a reputation for superb cuisine, a neat house and a love of beauty wherever she found it, Mary happily replaced her bonnet and plain clothes with a hat and some stylish clothing instead of the Dunkard garb when she cast her lot, too, with The Brethren Church. Her brother, A. D. Gnagey, was a leader in the reform movement and served as editor of *The Brethren Evangelist.*

For those history buffs who read small print, who verify dates and who note attributions, here are the 15 lines on Alva J. McClain's father which are entered in an encyclopedia of The Brethren Church:

McClain, Walter Scott (BC), 1861-1925, pastor,

farmer. Born in Masontown, PA, on March 1, W. S. McClain spent his early life in Pennsylvania and Iowa. He married Mary E. Gnagey in 1884. McClain joined the German Baptist Brethren at Waterloo, IA, in 1877, then affiliated with the Progressive Brethren (Brethren Church) in the division of 1882-83. He was ordained an elder in the Mt. Zion (Aurelia), IA, congregation in 1890. The McClains moved to Arizona Territory (1897) and to Los Angeles (1899) before settling near Sunnyside, WA, (1900). W. S. McClain operated a farm and nursery business. He preached occasionally and taught in the Sunnyside First Brethren Church Sunday school. He died July 8.

Walter always read the Bible at meal time and later, in his favorite chair, far into the evening as the children played about him. He looked upon the Good Book not only as a rule of faith but also as a book with principles for good health and long life. The more he read of Old Testament dietary exhortations the more he looked with suspicion upon those fat, succulent porkers out in his fields and upon the plates of chops, cracklins, puddin', and suet prepared by lard for his table. Hadn't the Lord clearly forbidden the partaking of such unclean food? As a painful object lesson, boils began to form on Father McClain's skin and "rheumatiz" stiffened his joints. At age 37, he was walking like a man twice his age.

Word spread among the congregation at Mt. Zion Brethren Church about good, flat acreage in the Territory of Arizona soon to be watered by irrigation from what is now the Roosevelt Dam. The news fell sweetly on Walter's ears. He closed his pig stables forever and turned west in an uncharacteristically sudden move.

In Aurelia, four of the seven McClain children had been born: Georgia Ada (1886); Alva Jay (1888); Arthur Stanley (1890), Mary Ellen (1892); and Leslie Daniel (1896). This was the family of Walter and Mary McClain as they headed west to the Arizona territory 13 years before it became a state. One member, sadly, was absent. Arthur, at the age of four, had been playing with Georgia and Alva inside the house when he fell against the railing of a crib and struck the base of his neck at the *medulla oblongota,* causing instant death. It was Arthur who loved to "preach" . . . Arthur who took out a leaf in the dining table, poured water into a tub on the floor, and solicited Georgia and Alva as play actors as he led a "baptismal" service which he had seen at church . . . Arthur who had caused his father more than once to suspect that perhaps he had held up the wrong child as "the preacher," and that he, like Isaac, should have crossed his hands and placed his blessing instead upon his third child. Now the little charmer was gone. Stoically, in acceptance of the will of God so characteristic of the Pennsylvania Dutch, the McClains laid their son in the soil of the Hawkeye State and went on.

Covered wagons, belching locomotives, and land, lots of land under starry skies above in 1898 greeted the McClains as they made the journey by rail and settled on an allotment of acreage which is now the city of Glendale, near Phoenix. Father McClain had worked hard in Aurelia, but he toiled harder still on the virgin soil of the Territory. William McKinley was President, Theodore Roosevelt the Vice President. A dam project up the Salt River northeasterly some 100 miles at Tortilla Flat, was on the federal drawing board but initiative was slow and precious water was running unused into the sea. What water might be available to the McClain ranch came at unexpected moments. In the middle of the night, occasionally, the hoofbeats of the "Paul Revere" of the Glendale Ranchers would pound up to the front door. The rider would call, "Water's a-comin'!" and Walter would rouse himself, put on his boots, grab his shovel and disappear into the night. This would happen also on the Lord's Day, causing the strict preacher to become more and more disenchanted with the vain struggle to coax crops from the hot sands of Arid-zona. He also began hearing discouraging words from neighbors about the dam in 1900.

"I'll bet it'll never be built . . . bet it's just talk!" they were saying. They little realized that President McKinley would be assassinated the following year and that the Rough Rider would take the helm as Commander-in-Chief and see to the building of the dam which today bears his name.

Alva, at 10, was making the most of the new frontier. He invited neighborhood buddies to his father's irrigation pond for a daily swim in the oppressive heat.

"We girls had to get away from there in the evening," his sister Mary recalls, "because Alva and his friends would go swimming in the nude."

Ruth Angeline had been born in 1898 on the Arizona ranch soon after they had arrived. Mother would soak the bed sheets in cold well water at bedtime so the children could get to sleep before the shimmering heat of the night could keep them awake.

At the turn of the century the world was at peace. The nation was getting used to saying "the twentieth century" as people ventured into the exciting further expansion of cities and farms on mountain and plain. Walter had not found in the Territory what he expected, so he once again sold out and moved west -- this time as far as he could go to bustling Los Angeles. He rented a rooming house at 131 North Broadway and purchased furniture to sub-let it to guests.

Alva adapted quickly to life in the city. He loved the easy access to books in a library nearby . . . enjoyed riding the street cars . . . spent a penny or two occasionally at the local drug store for some treats for his brother and sisters if he could pick up a job or two at the age of twelve . . . visited Union Station to watch the hissing monsters arriving from far away places with strange sounding names. Someday he would visit those cities.

Sitting in his easy chair one evening Father McClain leafed through his new copy of *The Brethren*

Evangelist and spotted a curious ad. Three midwestern pillars in the Brethren Church were calling for other families to join a Christian Cooperative Colony on the leeward side of the Cascade Mountains of Washington State at a place called Sunnyside. S. J. Harrison, H. M. Lichty, and Christian Rowland were gambling their future on the project. They had written into the charter a safeguard against the sale of alcoholic beverages, gambling, and vice of all kinds. If any participant were to yield to such temptations his deed would be returned to the colony and the holder restricted.

Walter McClain read the ad carefully and pondered the opportunity. The city, he had decided, was no place to raise a family. Out there on the acres of eastern Washington their feet could touch the virgin soil and their souls breathe in the fresh air of the country under the open face of heaven. Yes, the more he thought about it the more he liked the possibilities. "What could be more perfect?" he asked Mary. "A vice-free community where we can raise our children in a God-fearing society."

Mary pondered these things. She was not as enthusiastic as Walter, but in the spirit of her wedding vows she agreed that the matter was, at least, worth exploring.

Walter bought a rail ticket and left to see for himself. As his letters began arriving Mary knew their departure was only a matter of time. The content of her husband's letters could all be summed up in one vigorous, enthusiastic summons: "Come!"

3

Streams in the Desert

Shortly before the Christmas season of 1900, Mary suited up her brood once again for traveling and said good bye to her home for the third time in as many years. She had a premonition that this would be the last move until her family was raised and heaven would beckon. And she was right.

Picture the mother, her long skirts and elaborate hat, with five youngsters plus baby Fern Esther who had been born in L.A., embarking on her historic journey. Picture little Alva at 12, standing in shiny new boots at Union Station, watching the trains, looking after his sisters, asking questions, holding a cluster of books for the long train ride to a new life.

Picture the McClain youngsters vying for space at the windows of the Sante Fe to watch the passing land-scape as the train sped northward through the San

Joaquin Valley's orchards and vineyards and oceans of cotton . . . under the coastal redwood trees . . . transferring at Portland to the Northern Pacific Railroad line . . . speeding eastward through the Columbia River grandeur, excitement growing as they neared the rail stop called Mabton (a condensation of Mable Town named for a pioneering railroad man's daughter) eight miles south of Sunnyside where father would be waiting with a wagon and a team of horses.

Mary was shocked as she surveyed the dismal stretches of sand at Sunnyside interspersed by an occasional unpainted shack. She saw lizards, jackrabbits, coyotes and rattlesnakes but her husband's soft words were reassuring.

"Just wait," he told her. "This place is going to blossom like a rose."

In his eye of optimism he saw already the orchards of fruit that would make Washington apples famous, vineyards burdened with hanging grapes, fields of celery, asparagus, cauliflower, lettuce and cotton which would soon characterize the "Holy City" called Sunnyside.

It is not known what point of view young Alva McClain took as he rolled into town hanging onto the livery truck. Fewer than 300 dust-choked people lived in shacks that squatted on the blowsand, their dooryards devoid of grass or bloom or pavement.

The McClain family moved into the Sunnyside Hotel near the Northern Pacific Railroad tracks while a house was going up on Walter's 40 acres. The hotel was only six years old, but it had been built on sand and it was known to move in windy weather because its foundations consisted of a few rocks placed at intervals along its sills, not too deeply imbedded into the sandy earth. The ever-present winds had a playful habit of shifting the light soil from beneath the rocks to give the floor a peculiarly wavy appearance. The whole building would shake precariously when a severe gust would strike it broadside.

Alva McClain, quickly nicknamed "Mick" by Guy Lichty and other sons of the original pioneers, wrote no diary of those days but it is safe to conclude that the spirit of the boy responded to the challenge of this wilderness. He and Guy Lichty were seldom seen apart. What prank one boy overlooked the other quickly thought of.

Alva was required to attend church until he was sixteen. After that, his father promised, he was free to make his own decisions. The McClains worshipped first in a Federated Church at Seventh and Franklin Streets, a sanctuary shared by Presbyterians, Baptists, Methodists, and Congregationalists. The Brethren were first to build their own sanctuary at Sunnyside.

Occasionally Alva attended church in ways other than his parents had in mind. During services one evening, he and Guy decided to climb into the attic area above the sanctuary, make their way to the belfry and tie the rope to the bell so the custodian could not ring it. As they made their way along a dark passageway they were spotted by an earth-bound parishioner so haste was required to carry out the errant mission. Guy lost his footing, stepped accidentally on an unsupported part of the ceiling, and fell through. The congregation looked up in time to see a foot dangling wildly through the roof. Guy's father, H. M. Lichty, recognized at once his son's new shoes and knew who the guilty party was. He also knew he would be with Alva on the mischievous errand. For many years, people throughout the Brethren church told the story incorrectly that Alva McClain's foot had come through the ceiling. In a telephone conversation in mid-December, 1985, Earl Campbell told the author: "The patch is still there. I saw it at worship service just this morning."

Alva often told his wife: "I can't understand why that mis-step has been consistently blamed on me!"

His sisters found it easy to explain. When mischief was going on in Sunnyside, their brother was usually behind it.

On April 11, 1905 when Alva turned sixteen, he made his choice. He would leave churchgoing to his parents and sisters. He had more interesting things to do -- things like playing football and baseball, smoking cigarettes with his chums, dancing at the town hall, and playing cards. Whatever he tried he mastered. He took his sister Mary to a dance several times but she didn't care for it.

"We're going to dance in heaven," a friend told her years later.

"Well, if we do," Mary replied, "I won't know how."

Mick liked to ride to Mabton with Guy and his father where the senior Lichty met newcomers on inbound trains. It was Lichty's job to try to persuade the families to stay. Their natural inclination often was to get right back on the train and return to civilization. If he could get them to Sunnyside, Mrs. Lichty would hospitably entertain them. She had a cheerful disposition, offered good food, and shared her enthusiasm for Sunnyside as each prospective citizen considered staying.

The McClain kids attended first the one-room Emerson schoolhouse, the only painted building in Sunnyside, and later Denny Blaine School. The school system added a grade a year and thus tried to keep ahead of the enlarging population.

In school, Alva heard the story often of how Sunnyside came to be. It had all begun a couple of decades before the McClains arrived when President Thomas F. Oakes of the Northern Pacific Railroad Company noted the exceptional crops being produced on garden-sized tracts, just south of Union Gap. A few settlers had ditched a trickle of water from the river to irrigate them, producing phenomenal results. Oakes had a mental picture of a canal carrying water to his company's arid acres to convert them into a verdant, productive paradise, incidentally creating huge tonnage for his railroad to carry to cities on the coast. Was it an impracticable dream? Such a project would be the largest of its kind yet attempted! Was it feasible? He'd investigate. He sent for the only engineer with irrigation experience, Walter N. Granger, who'd built some small experimental projects in Montana.

Impressed by what Oakes told him about crops grown and the broad valley of volcanic soil needing only water to duplicate the miracle he'd seen in garden-size plots, Granger boarded the train for Yakima City (now Union Gap) for a look. He hired a Cayuse (Indian pony) and horsebacked into the lower Yakima Valley. Reaching Snipes Mountain, he climbed to its crest for the better view it offered. Following its ridge to the eastern end he reached conclusions to be made a part of history's records:

> The vast area of practically level land below us plainly indicated that we were in the heart of the region. As I gazed on the scene I then and there resolved that a city should some day be built at the base of the mountain for the site was ideal.

Although it had no name then, the site of Sunnyside was determined before it was certain a canal would ever be built, a full year before its route was located and surveyed, three years before a canal was built as far as Zillah and five years before irrigation water reached Sunnyside and a townsite surveyed and plotted, in 1894.

For five years Granger worked. He optioned 90,000 acres of railroad land from the railroad company at $1.25 per acre; he formed a company to finance, build, and operate the Sunnyside Canal. He located and surveyed its route and lateral system . . . organized, surveyed and plotted two townsites -- Zillah and Sunnyside . . . established and built offices at Zillah . . . and had water running in his Sunnyside Canal all the forty miles to its end in 1894, Black Rock Canyon east of Sunnyside.

His irrigation company had gone broke, but Granger kept water flowing for the few settlers who hung on by their eyelashes. He printed "funny money" to finance the project until a reorganization was effected. Most of the early settlers in Sunnyside threw up their hands in despair and left. The townsite was claimed through foreclosure by the mortgage company which had advanced money for its development. Seven families stayed as the critical year of 1898 arrived.

"Get the Brethren," Granger said. "They know how to work and they believe you when you tell them about the possibilities here."

At this point in the story the McClains became part of Sunnyside's history. Fellow Iowans arrived steadily. The William Hitchcock family settled in Sunnyside in 1901. Hitchcock had published a newspaper in Colfax before succumbing to the lure of a planned community. He established the town's first newspaper, the *Sunnyside Sun*, and published its first issue on May 24, 1901. Church services were first held in Emerson Grade School.

Thirty hand-cranking, battery-powered telephones connected by a single wire carried on fence posts were available. Streets and roads were wagon tracks through sagebrush. A dug well, equipped with an "old oaken bucket," where each citizen furnished the power for rope-over-pulley domestic water system, supplied the town. Lighting was accomplished by kerosene lamp or lantern, electricity being something reserved for large cities. It was for Sunnyside at this time only a wispy dream.

Transportation was available by two methods only: horse power or "shanks mare." Automobiles, even though there would have been a place to drive them, were conspicuously absent. They were but "a passing fad," merely "a richman's toy."

The eight McClains soon moved into the house father built on the ranch. From there they moved to the "Lutheran Place" which they rented, thence to the "Rankin Place" which had a separate house for Mother's kitchen, then to a house beside the railroad tracks and finally to "the old Yoder Place" which Walter bought and in which both he and his wife died in 1925 and 1920 respectively.

The McClain youngsters were having too much fun to notice privations. An outhouse with the outdated Sears Roebuck catalog served just fine. As long as mother could fry those delicious potatoes in cottolene oil (lard had been long since outlawed in the McClain home) they would never want for tasty food. Alva once ordered a plate of his mother's fried potatoes in lieu of a birthday cake.

Alva referred to his younger sisters, Ruth and Fern as "the kids." Occasionally he would give them a dime if he could earn a little surplus working on the farm and later in his father's fruit orchards. He also knew how to get their goat. One evening Georgia decided to invite her girl friends to a slumber party on father's flattened haystack next to the barn. Alva noted that they climbed a ladder to their lofty perch and so before dawn, he sneaked out and removed it.

As the sun rose next day and the breakfast bell sounded, no girls appeared.

"That's funny," Mother said to herself in the kitchen. "The girls should have been here long ago."

When he thought the angry cries of Georgia had gone on long enough, Alva replaced the ladder for his sister and her uncomfortable guests.

With good fortune came the bad. Father bought a pedigreed horse the children named "Belle" who quickly became part of the family. Alva loved her wide, smooth back and could gallop across the ranch at full tilt. They intended to raise a colt from her but Father loaned the horse to a friend where Belle took sick. She later died before she could leave behind her equestrian offspring, and so another dream died with her. Alva later had a pair of Cayuses of his own and taught them tricks.

Mick McClain and Guy Lichty explored the peaks of Big Snipes Mountain . . . played pick-up games of football on sand lots . . . organized baseball teams in the spring . . . and skipped school as often as they could. Familiar to his surviving sisters is their mother's plaintive reply to a teacher on the telephone: "But I *sent* him to school this morning!"

The McClain children suffered together when their father read long Bible passages before they could dive into the savory appetizers of their mother at meal time. A pledge of honor extracted from mischievous Alva gave the rest of the family some measure of privacy on Saturday nights as each took his turn in the tub. They also shared childhood diseases, including small pox, scarlet fever, and even the seven-year itch which Ruth remembers quarantined them and required (on orders from mother) the swallowing of a horrible potion sometimes mercifully camouflaged in applesauce or cake frosting.

Bib overalls do not a farmer make. Alva was happier racing his Cayuses or quarterbacking for his high school team, or running the bases on the sand lot ball team. He hated most working the bees. His father never got stung, but no matter how Alva bundled up he was never able to convince the bees that he was their friend, and someone not to be bitten. He concluded that if a person is afraid of them he gives off an odor which the bees detect and which causes them to attack.

None of the four houses had indoor plumbing. Water had to be carried in, but it drained out through pipes into cesspools.

To settle an argument with Mary one day, Alva let loose ol' Ramikins, a pet goat that had turned mean. Mary had time to climb a pole where he let her sit until he had proved his point. The "point" has been long forgotten, but the opportunity for some good laughs has not been.

Big brother Alva often made Sister Ruth laugh so hard she had to leave the table to get control of herself. Alva taught his sisters to dance the two-step, the brand new three-step, and some waltzes, but he would not have tolerated their learning to smoke as he had.

For three years his quarterbacking on the high school football team held the Yakima Valley championships. In later years Mick remarked to a friend as they were watching a football game, "They've spoiled the game with so many rules."

"I think," said Mrs. McClain with a chuckle, "that Alva and his buddies made up some of the rules as they went along."

Perhaps she was right. One day his teammates scored by snapping the ball to Mick then grabbing him and throwing him with the ball over the line of scrimmage and the lunging enemy right into the end zone.

One autumn when the apples were harvested and football had replaced orchard work, Mick left on a three-day trip with his team, playing in scheduled games all over the valley. When he came home he fell into bed and could not be wakened the next morning. No amount of noise, shaking, or calling could bring him back to consciousness. He remembered those days fondly in later years when insomnia plagued him.

"Getting Alva up in the morning," Ruth recalls, "took about an hour. Father once took the door off its hinges to get into his room and waken him. I always hated to make his bed. The coverings were always twisted into an impossible mess. Took me half an hour just to untangle the sheets."

Georgia, two years older than her brother, worked hard in school while Mick loafed and still caught up with her by skipping grades. Although he loved to read, he did not pay much attention to class schedules. It was more fun to play ball.

A teacher at Sunnyside High School named Mr. Oliphant was angered by Mick's sporadic attendance. He was determined that he wouldn't graduate with his class. Another teacher, a Miss Allen, was equally determined that Alva J. McClain was indeed going to graduate. Father and Mother McClain on the sidelines were cheering for their son because they were of the opinion that anyone who had a high school diploma could make his way successfully in whatever pursuit he chose.

A series of special tests were devised and submitted to young Alva. If he passed them he would graduate; if he failed, he would have to take the year over again. On the day of the tests, Mr. Oliphant sat down beside Alva to watch every step. But Alva had read the books from which the questions were taken (his sisters think he read the books the evening before) and knew the answers. On graduation evening, Miss Allen and the McClains sat in the audience, proud and content, while Mr. Oliphant went upstairs and played the piano in a pout.

In 1908, Mick left home for the University of Washington. His interest in higher education at that time was placed second to sports. He was soon the school's quarterback and also a member of the baseball team. His budding career in sports ended one day in 1909 when he was racing for first base as an opposing team player was walking backward to catch the ball. The collision resulted in a spike penetrating Mick's leg and sending him to the hospital. There is no record of any sports activity after that accident. Blood poisoning threatened to take his life, and the shin bone became so soft it felt like putty. He went home to recuperate and never returned to the University of Washington.

Father and Mother McClain had their own special nursing techniques for their children. Mother leaned toward concoctions; father trusted in manipulation and techniques developed by osteopathy. Both trusted in the Lord to deliver.

The year Alva came home from the Huskies, his father and H. M. Lichty organized the Yakima-Sunnyside Nursery Company to grow only pedigree fruit trees. A certificate was issued with each purchase, stating the location and production record of the parent tree. Alva joined his father in the nursery business at the age of 20 years. As far as he knew, this would be his life's career. He became skilled in planting, pruning, and budding the fine apple trees of the now-famous Yakima Valley. Apple seeds, planted in the summer, would come up as seedlings. Alva would select from mature apple trees buds which he would skillfully graft onto the seedling. Thousands of bud sticks passed through his hands as he raised and sold the precious prunage.

The process was simple, yet demanding. It was told to many a congregation and to many a class in later years as he weaved it into sermon illustrations. Nurseryman Alva would select from mature apple trees buds which he would skillfully graft onto the seedling. Very carefully he would cut a slit in the branch one direction and then another, making a cross on the surface skin. The bud, then, would be slipped just behind the skin of the apple tree where it would start to grow. Later, the top of the seedling was cut off and the tree was on its way. His sisters would come behind him and gently tie the buds to the branch so that they'd have a firm connection with the mother branch.

Alva spotted on Nob Hill one day a Rome Beauty apple without the characteristic green stripes -- just pure red ones. The freakish fruit was a kind of mutation that grew accidentally. Alva went back in a hurry with tools and took some bud sticks for his own orchard business. Today one seldom sees any other kind of Rome Beauty than ones like the sport he found on the slopes of Sunnyside so many years ago.

4

New Pathways

By 1910, the reclamation project at Sunnyside was in full swing. Mountains spouted dust as machines cut and scraped the virgin soil . . . canals sliced through its valleys reaching thirsty fields and orchards. Reclamation projects attract engineers, and in those days most were young marriageable men fresh from university classrooms. It was no secret that marriageable women might do well to settle in Sunnyside.

Mick turned 22 on April 11. His thoughts, as he cut buds for new trees, shoveled fertilizer, trimmed trees, guided irrigation water or sacked sawdust at the nursery, were focused passionately on sports and reading. He dated a few Sunnyside belles but no one claimed his attention for long. The son of the lay preacher clung to his fondness for dancing, cards, and cigarettes. It is a credit to Walter that he did not alienate his son -- this child who was to be the preacher of the family -- or anger him by trying to do the work of the Holy Spirit. Instead, the two went into the nursery business together.

Back in Iowa, Josephine Gingrich turned nineteen, that year. She and her sister Velora had left home three years earlier after graduating from La Porte City High School to enter the Iowa State Teachers College (now the University of Northern Iowa) in Cedar Falls. Jo became homesick and her sister's bronchial condition worsened at Cedar Falls. A few weeks into the first semester the two packed their bags, bought a one-way ticket on the train and returned to their parents and other sisters, Lucille and Catherine. Shortly afterward, a new business college was organized in Waterloo called the Waterloo College of Commerce. Father Gingrich bought two "scholarships" so that Jo and Velora could attend and live at home.

Jo graduated in 1910 at the age of 19 with skills in bookkeeping. She tested the waters in hometown La Porte City in Benton County but no suitable employment presented itself. At this choice moment, a letter arrived from Roscoe Sheller in Sunnyside, a family friend. He invited Josephine and Velora to put their talents to work in the office of the Sunnyside Reclamation Project. A Mr. Webster lived next door to the Shellers. When he found out that Jo had accepted Weller's invitation he arranged for the new girl to meet "a special friend." That friend was Alva J. McClain.

No one could arrive in a small town like Sunnyside -- especially a woman -- unnoticed. Since the McClains lived near the train track Jo was noticed as soon as she stepped off the Northern Pacific's scheduled steamer. It came as quite a surprise at the dinner table one evening when Alva asked, "Well, have you seen my new girl?"

Father and Mother laid down their forks in surprise.

"Yes," Mary piped up. "I saw her. She passed me on the street with her nose in the air."

Alva laughed. "She's just proper, that's all."

"Where is she from?" Mother wanted to know.

"Waterloo. La Porte City, really. She's good Iowa stock, just like us."

Josephine Gingrich, standing little more than five feet tall, was indeed "good Iowa stock" like most of the McClain children but she was unlike them in her lack of a spiritual heritage. Georgia, Mary, Ruth, and Fern had little hope for the relationship. They were certain that when Jo found out about their prankster brother . . . about his dancing . . . his addiction to cigarettes . . . and about his passion for sports, she would drop him. But Miss Gingrich had eyes to see in young McClain something deep. He was always a gentleman, always polite, soft-spoken and quick. In August, 1910, they became engaged and were married the following year on June 7.

Jo continued to work during her engagement in the Sunnyside Abstract and Title Company, moving up to a responsible position as secretary to the boss. She was paid $50 a month in gold, and by June she had a nest egg saved to contribute to the marriage.

They slipped away to Yakima on that historic Saturday morning, fifty miles to the north, where they found an Episcopal pastor who would perform the ceremony. Alva's friend, Guy Lichty, witnessed the union and saw the happy pair off to Seattle for a brief honeymoon. Even though both were secular in their pursuits at the beginning, their marriage was made in heaven and lasted for 57 years until the groom's death at 80 in 1968. No wife ever supported her husband more faithfully than Mrs. McClain. Said she in a classic understatement: "I was always interested in whatever he was doing."

At the end of the honeymoon, Alva returned home apprehensively. He had participated in so many mischievous chivarees for his friends who had been married that he dreaded what they in turn were now prepared to carry out in revenge. He and Jo moved into Mother and Father McClain's big house and were given an upstairs room.

One night, as Mick had predicted, it happened. Chums invaded, sneaking into the honeymoon suite when the newlyweds were out. Jo had hung a fishnet on the south wall and displayed on it the greeting cards from friends. Gifts had been arranged on tables, pictures hung, and a new bedspread placed on the bed. By the time the invaders left, the room was quite different.

"It looks like the ruins of Rome," Mary moaned as she peeked in.

The bed sheets were hopelessly knotted, the bed dismantled, the fishnet tangled, draperies unhung, and gifts strewn. The pranks of Mick McClain and the people he had tormented all in good fun were finally avenged.

In late August of 1912, Pastor W. S. Bell of the Sunnyside Brethren Church invited a popular speaker named Louis S. Bauman to be the featured evangelist in a week-long Bible conference. On Monday morning, the first day of the scheduled series, Walter suggested casually to his son, "Why don't you take off work this afternoon and go hear Bauman down at the church?"

Alva thought it over. Why not? He hadn't been inside the church for half a decade at least. At lunch he talked it over with Jo. They decided to go together. Nothing to lose. Might even be interesting.

The young couple, married a year and three months, walked to the church in their Sunday best. Alva smoked a cigarette on the way, taken from the silver case his wife had given him for a wedding gift. They took their places among the pews, sang the hymns perfunctorily, and no doubt set some tongues to wagging. Nothing would come from the pulpit, Alva was certain, which he hadn't heard before.

L. S. Bauman preached that day on his favorite subject -- biblical prophecy. As Alva listened he leaned forward intently. *Imagine,* he thought, *a God who can write history ahead of time and put the events of tomorrow into a book before they arrived.*

That evening Mick and Jo were back for more. When the sermon ended and the preacher made his appeal for unbelievers to make a commitment to follow Jesus Christ Alva turned to Jo and whispered, "I'm going down there."

"Can I go with you?" she asked, standing up quickly and walking with her husband as he hurried to the altar. The evening was eventful: two people were born again; a lifelong friendship was begun between the evangelist and the nurseryman, and the lives of the newlyweds were headed in a new direction. Another "prophecy" of a sort was fulfilled that day. Walter McClain, who had had eyes of faith when he held up his new son and predicted, "Here is our preacher," at last saw his faith become sight.

On the way home from church, Alva reached into his pocket and took out his cigarettes. "I won't need these anymore," he said, emptying his silver case into a trash can. They were easily discarded but quitting was agony. His lungs screamed for nicotine in his silent battle to overcome. Jo knew, but none of the family was aware of Mick's battle to kick the habit which had become entrenched so early.

Alva took up his father's habit of reading the Bible in the evening at home. L. S. Bauman had told the elders, "Watch the little fellow." Books became not merely entertainment to be sandwiched into a busy schedule but pathways to knowledge of the Scriptures. The Bible began to make sense. Prophecy became exciting instead of dull. The Gospels became the biography of His Savior and the Epistles his new rule of faith and practice on which to build his marriage and his career.

5

Wingspread

As a Christian, Alva found the old cliches coming true: the sky seemed more blue, the grass a bit greener, the prospect for the future brighter. The news of Alva's homecoming raced through the family network. His mother's brother, Uncle A. D. Gnagey who had been a leader in the organization of the Brethren Church, must have reminded the new Christian that his father and mother had long prayed for the Hound of Heaven to overtake him. Pastor W. S. Bell at the Sunnyside Brethren Church had the pleasure of baptizing Alva and Jo. Some of their worldly friends came to watch. They predicted "it" wouldn't last.

"You, a Christian?" they guffawed.

"It's true," Mick would reply, "and you need the Lord, too."

Alva lost friends when he became a Christian but

he gained many new ones. And some of his former friends were later reconciled.

No more Sunday baseball. Now Alva and Jo entered enthusiastically into the service of the local church. Alva sang in the choir and lent his baritone voice to a male quartet.

"Whenever the church doors were opened," Mrs. McClain recalls, "he was there."

Alva lost the desire to return to the University of Washington to complete his education. Instead, he wanted to follow L. S. Bauman to Long Beach where the evangelist had been called to establish the church which became the First Brethren Church, referred to by its members as "Fifth and Cherry" (from its address a few blocks from the ocean). Alva's fondest wish was now to sit at the feet of the one who had introduced him to his Lord.

On their second wedding anniversary, June 7, 1913, Alva and Jo got their chance. They packed their belongings and left Sunnyside for Long Beach, never to live again in the place where Alva had grown to manhood. At the suggestion of Dr. Bauman, Alva enrolled for Bible training at The Bible Institute of Los Angeles -- a school built with funds supplied by Lyman Stewart, founder and president of Union Oil Company, and made prominent by the world famous theologian, Reuben Archer Torrey.

For 10 golden months, from September 1914, until the following June, the nurseryman immersed himself in Bible study. Like Jacob whose seven years of service for Rachel seemed but a few days because of his love for his bride, the year at Biola seemed but a few days because of his love for the Bible.

After a year in Los Angeles, Alva wanted more intensive theological training. He inquired of Dr. Bauman what seminary he might enter and was advised that there was none better than Xenia Theological Seminary, an institution of the United Presbyterian Church, in Xenia, Ohio. Dr. William G.

Moorhead, a Bible teacher and archeologist of global fame, was the president. Dr. Bell, his pastor in Sunnyside, strongly advised Alva to attend Ashland College's Bible program "where you could get both sides of theological questions."

"I already know which side I'm on," Alva countered. Later he advised students: "Study where you can trust the faculty. When you eat ice cream you want to enjoy it, not worry about how much arsenic is in it."

To Xenia Alva would go. It seems strange now that the strong young football player would make the trip alone to Ohio to see if he could endure the severe winters of the Buckeye State. It seemed that when he became converted, the Devil attacked his body. He was to battle precarious health for the rest of his life through half a dozen major operations, a year of annoying vertigo, and finally Parkinson's disease.

Joined later by his wife in Ohio, Alva finished at Xenia in 1917 his work toward a Th.M. degree but would be awarded it upon his completion of his B.A. degree. He had commuted by interurban trains to Yellow Springs, Ohio, to take studies at Antioch College, but eight years later he would graduate from Occidental College in Los Angeles with highest honors and receive in one day both his B.A. and his Th.M. degrees. While studying at Antioch, he served as student pastor with a circuit of three Brethren churches at Clayton, Miamisburg, and Dayton.

At the 1917 National Conference in Ashland, Ohio, he was ordained to the Brethren ministry and elected to membership in the Foreign Mission Board. His special supervision was the new field in French Equatorial Africa, later to become (after the country gained its independence) the Central African Republic.

A representative from the First Brethren Church of Philadelphia was at the 1917 National Conference. He urged the new preacher to consider becoming the pastor of First Brethren Church in Philadelphia whose pulpit was empty. Alva visited the church, spoke several times to the congregation, and promised to consider their invitation in 1918, the following year, after he had finished his commitment at the three student churches.

A year later the Philadelphia church called again. This time he was ready to make the move, right in the middle of the Second World War. Housing was in short supply, and the church had no parsonage so the McClains were entertained by Mrs. Anna McArthur and her daughter Alice.

A love affair between the pastor and his people developed in the City of Brotherly Love. Warm are the memories of those who were in that church. While Jo saw to the arrangements for housing, Alva poured his time into study and preaching, and the general work of a spiritual shepherd.

When a house next to the church was put on the market, the McClains borrowed money for a downpayment and moved in. Keeping up the payments on their first house with a pastor's salary was hard. In 1919 they sold the house and made enough on the sale for the young pastor to pay off the money borrowed for the downpayment, to pay also a school debt, and for Alva to make a trip to Sunnyside to visit his mother who was terminally ill.

On his way to his Philadelphia parish each morning the young pastor watched the people and observed the street signs en route. On the outside of a woodworking shop he read, "All Kinds of Twisting and Turning Done Here."

"That," Alva told his people in a sermon, "could be said of many a modernistic church in this city today."

One day several young men made an appointment to see their pastor. The matter was their decision to join the Masonic Lodge.

"Is is biblical?" one asked.

Another wanted to know, "Are you in favor of it?"

The third asked, "Would it enhance our testimony for Christ?"

Pastor McClain pondered their questions. He had his views of Masonry but felt it would not be fair to lay it on the young men without further research.

"Tell you what," he proposed. "I'll research the subject and preach a sermon on my findings. You'll know where I stand by listening to the sermon. I'll not say any more about it after that."

Rev. McClain made a fair investigation of Masonry on the basis of such literature as was available to the general public. Here is the famous sermon -- a message that would follow him to the campus of his church's denominational college and on through the generations in a printed tract which is more true today, some say, than when it was first preached:

MASONRY AND CHRISTIANITY

I have two texts: Matthew 12:30 -- "He that is not with me is against me"; John 12:48 -- "He that rejecteth me, and receiveth not my words, hath one that judgeth him: the word that I have spoken, the same shall judge him in the last day."

Will you listen carefully while I present three propositions?

1. Jesus Christ is God manifest in the flesh, and apart from Him the true God can neither be known, worshiped, nor acknowledged.

2. Salvation is by faith in the atoning blood of the Lord Jesus Christ apart from all human works and character.

3. It is the supreme obligation of every saved person to obey the Lord Jesus Christ in all things.

These three propositions are the pillars of the Christian faith -- the deity of Christ; salvation by faith in Him; obedience to His Word. Do you believe these three things? I am going to ask every person who does to stand! (Nearly the entire congregation stood.) Thank you. I knew you believed them, but I can preach to you better after that testimony.

About four weeks ago I called over the telephone

one of the highest officers of the Grand Lodge, at his office at the Masonic Temple in Philadelphia. I told him frankly that I was not a Mason and that I desired to obtain some authentic information regarding Freemasonry and its religious position. This officer suggested three books by Masonic authorities. I told him that one would be sufficient, and asked him which of the three books was the best. Without hesitation he answered, "Get the *Encyclopedia of Freemasonry,* by Mackey. It is, without question, our highest and best authority."

He then referred me to a man at the Masonic Library. I called him and asked him for the highest and most authentic Masonic authority. Without a moment's hesitation he answered, "Get the *Encyclopedia of Freemasonry,* by Mackey." I have that encyclopedia with me here tonight. In the main, my analysis of Freemasonry shall be based upon its statements and claims. Surely, no Mason can question the fairness of this method.

The author of this encyclopedia, Albert G. Mackey, is one of Masonry's most learned and famous men. Besides being a Thirty-Second Degree Mason, he held many high offices in the organization. At the writing of this work he was "Past General Grand High Priest of the General Grand Chapter of the United States." Practically his whole life was devoted to research work on behalf of Masonry. His industry was amazing! A stream of books came from his pen, among which is *A Lexicon of Freemasonry, Manual of the Lodge, The Book of the Chapter, A Text Book of Masonic Jurisprudence, Cryptic Masonry, The Symbolism of Masonry,* and *The Masonic Ritualist.* This encyclopedia, however, is the crowning work of his life. He was engaged in its preparation for 30 years.

This encyclopedia contains about a thousand pages, with articles upon almost every conceivable subject that is in any way related to Freemasonry. During the past four weeks I have gone through the book carefully and have read hundreds of its articles. I am impressed with the exhaustive manner with which the author treats the various subjects.

Certainly I am not in agreement with the doctrines of the institution which Dr. Mackey defends, but that does not keep me from admiring his able scholarship, his painstaking research work, his sober and fair presentation of Masonic subjects. And my admiration increases when I remember the extreme difficulty under which Dr. Mackey was compelled to prepare his encyclopedia. The authors and editors of other encyclopedias never faced such a difficulty. Dr. Mackey was expected to give to the public the fullest possible exposition of Masonry and at the same time reveal none of its *secret work*. In spite of this difficulty, Mackey has produced a monumental work and all Masons may justly point to the man with pride.

My examination of Freemasonry tonight will be absolutely from the viewpoint of a Christian. I have nothing to say to Masons who are not Christians. If I were not a Christian, I would undoubtedly be a Mason tonight, as I was preparing to enter when the Lord Jesus saved my soul. I am speaking to those who own Jesus Christ as Lord and God.

I shall not assume to speak for Freemasonry tonight -- *Freemasonry shall speak for itself.* By its own utterances, by its own words, Freemasonry must stand justified or condemned. Matthew 12:37 -- "For by thy words thou shalt be justified, and by thy words thou shalt be condemned."

I. MASONRY CLAIMS TO BE A RELIGIOUS INSTITUTION

This claim is made not once in this encyclopedia, but literally dozens of times in different articles. We have not the time to hear all these references. I shall ask you to hear only one. Under the articles on *Religion*, Dr. Mackey discusses fully the right of Masonry to be called a "religious institution." He says that some of the more "timid brethren" have been afraid to declare its religious character lest the opponents of Masonry should use this fact against the lodge. But he insists that the truth should be told. I quote from the encyclopedia (pp. 618-619):

> "I contend, without any sort of hesitation, that Masonry is, in every sense of the word except one, and that its least philosophical, an eminently religious institution -- that it is indebted solely to the religious element which it contains for its origin and for its continued existence, and that without this religious element it would scarcely be worthy of cultivation by the wise and good. But, that I may be truly understood, it will be well first to agree upon the true definition of religion. There is nothing more illogical than to reason upon undefined terms."

Dr. Mackey then gives, in full, Webster's definition of "religion." The quotation is too lengthy to give in full, but Dr. Mackey proves conclusively that Freemasonry meets every requirement of Webster's three primary definitions of religion, and sums up the proof in the following words:

> "Look at its ancient landmarks, its sublime ceremonies, its profound symbols and allegories -- all inculcating religious doctrine, commanding religious observance, and teaching religious truth, and who can deny that it is eminently a religious institution?
> "Masonry, then, is indeed a religious institution; and on this ground mainly, if not alone, should the religious Mason defend it."

This should settle for all time the question as to whether or not Freemasonry is religious. According to its own claims, it is proper to speak of the "religion of Freemasonry." The man who contends that Freemasonry is not a "religious institution" is childishly ignorant of the organization or else he is a willful deceiver! Masonry is religious -- it teaches religion. But this fact does not necessarily condemn Freemasonry.

Now I desire to lay down a Biblical truth -- an axiom of Christianity. Here it is: *There is only ONE true religion. That religion is Christianity. All other religions are false.*

I need not argue that proposition. No Christian has ever denied it. But listen to the word of the Lord Jesus himself on this point. Jesus said, "I am the door." The door to what? The door to God; the door to heaven; the door to eternal life. But that is not all. Listen to this same Jesus as He continues: "All that ever came before me are thieves and robbers" (John 10:7-8).

We are now in a position where we can determine absolutely whether or not the religion of Freemasonry is false or true. Here are the propositions:

There is but one true religion -- Christianity!
Freemasonry has a religion!
If it is Christianity, it is true!
If it is not Christianity, it is false!

The issue is perfectly clear. The logic of these propositions cannot be evaded. We shall now go to Masonry's highest authority and say: "You have told us that your institution is a religious institution. We believe you, but we would ask you one more question. 'Is your religion Christianity or is it not Christianity?'" Freemasonry has answered this question. Mark carefully the answer on page 618 of the encyclopedia:

"The religion of Freemasonry . . . is not Christianity."

These are not *my* words! They are the words of Masonry's own encyclopedia, prepared by one of the greatest Masonic authors, recommended to me as authentic by one of the highest officers of the Grand Lodge in Philadelphia! It declares Freemasonry has a religion, and that religion is not Christianity!

I have not condemned Freemasonry. Freemasonry has condemned itself.

Let us use a little logic here: If the religion of Freemasonry is not Christianity, then it is false. If the religion of Freemasonry is false, then it is not of God! If the religion of Freemasonry is not of God, then it is of the evil one!

Does any man care to stand up and say that a Christian can belong to and support an institution which teaches a religion which is not Christianity? If so, let him face the Apostle Paul, who said: "But though we, or an angel from heaven, preach any other gospel unto you than that which we have preached unto you, let him be accursed. As we said before, so say I now again, if any man preach any other gospel unto you than that ye have received, let him be accursed" (Gal. 1:8-9). The curse of God is upon every religion outside of Christianity.

I might pronounce the benediction and go home, but there is more to be said.

II. FREEMASONRY RATES CHRISTIANITY AS A 'SECTARIAN RELIGION' WHILE BOASTING OF ITS OWN 'UNIVERSALITY.'

Again I quote from the encyclopedia:

"The religion of Masonry is not sectarian. It admits men of every creed within its hospitable bosom, rejecting none and approving none for his peculiar faith. It is not Judaism . . . it is not Christianity . . ." (p. 619).

"It does not meddle with sectarian creeds or doctrines, but teaches fundamental religious truth" (p. 618).

"If Masonry were simply a Christian institution, the Jew and the Moslem, the Brahman and the Buddhist, could not conscientiously partake of its illumination; but its universality is its boast. In its language, citizens of every nation may converse. At its altar men of all religions may kneel. To its creed, disciples of every faith may subscribe" (p. 439).

I came here tonight determined to discuss this subject of Masonry deliberately and calmly, but I find it difficult in the face of the audacious blasphemy of such statements and claims as I have read! Can you, as a Christian, sit unmoved by such a dastardly comparison between Christianity and Masonry? According to this noted Masonic authority, Christianity is a sectarian religion. Christianity can be compared with

Mohammedanism, Buddhism, and Brahmanism! Masonry cannot be compared to these religions. Christianity teaches a sectarian creed. Masonry teaches a creed of fundamental religious truth.

Do I need to tell this audience that all these great swelling words are a lie? If you want the truth, just reverse all these statements. It is the religion of Masonry that is sectarian. Christianity is the universal religion. It is the religion of Masonry that belongs down in the market place alongside of Buddhism, Brahmanism, and Mohammedanism. Christianity belongs above them all!

Oh, you Christians here tonight, is our Christ only a sectarian Christ, deserving only of a place alongside of these false prophets? Is that blessed faith which He came to inaugurate by His sinless life, His atoning death, His resurrection from the dead -- is this faith, after all, only a sectarian faith like that of Mohammed and Buddha? I tell you, *No!* But let the Bible answer.

"I saw in the night visions, and behold, one like the Son of man came with the clouds of heaven, and came to the Ancient of days, and they brought him near before him. And there was given him dominion, and glory, and a kingdom, that all people, nations, and languages, should serve him: his dominion is an everlasting dominion, which shall not pass away, and his kingdom that which shall not be destroyed" (Dan. 7:13-14).

"Behold the Lamb of God, which taketh away *the sin of the world*" (John 1:29).

"And I, if I be lifted up from the earth, will draw *all men unto me* (John 12:32).

"He is the propitiation for our sins: and not for ours only, but also for the sins of the *whole world*" (I John 2:2).

"Wherefore God also hath highly exalted him, and given him a name which is above every name: that at the name of Jesus *every knee* should bow . . . and that *every tongue* should confess that Jesus Christ is Lord, to the glory of God the Father" (Phil. 2:9-11).

III. MASONRY DOES NOT CONFESS JESUS CHRIST AS LORD AND GOD. THEREFORE, THE GOD OF MASONRY IS NOT THE TRUE GOD.

Masonry has a god -- you can't have a religion without a god. And this god has a name. Over and over in this encyclopedia you meet with the initials "G.A.O.T.U." This is the god of Masonry. The initials stand for the name "Great Architect of the Universe." This is the god that the Masons worship at their altar. This is the god to whom Masonic prayers are offered. Sometimes other names are applied to him, but, according to Mackey, "G.A.O.T.U." is the technical Masonic name for him (p. 290, 310).

Now I shall present the Christian view of God. Every intelligent Christian is acquainted with it, but let us refresh our minds. I shall present it in three statements:

(1) *There is only one true God.* This one true God exists in three Persons -- Father, Son, and Holy Spirit! But there are not three Gods. There is only one God, indivisible in substance and being.

(2) *This one true God became incarnate in the flesh and is none other than Jesus Christ.*

"In the beginning was the Word, and the Word was with God, and the Word was God . . . And the Word was made flesh, and dwelt among us, (and we beheld his glory, the glory as of the only begotten of the Father,) full of grace and truth" (John 1:1,14) . . .

(3) *The one true God cannot be confessed, honored, acknowledged, worshiped, believed on, or prayed to, apart from Jesus Christ!*

"Whosoever denieth the son, the same hath not the Father . . ." (I John 2:23).

This is the Christian doctrine of God. Let me sum it up briefly: There is one true God. This true God is revealed in the Person of Jesus Christ. Apart from Christ there is no true God. If a man confesses Jesus Christ, he is confessing the true God. If he worships

Jesus Christ, he is worshiping the true God. If a man refuses to confess Jesus Christ as God, he is denying the true God. If he refuses to worship Jesus Christ, he is refusing to worship the true God.

Now we are ready for the question, "Is the god of Masonry the true God, or is he a false god?"

The answer depends absolutely upon Masonry's attitude toward Jesus Christ. If Masonry asks its initiates to acknowledge and confess Jesus Christ as Lord and the true God, then Masonry's god is the true God. But if Masonry does not require its members to confess and acknowledge Jesus Christ as Lord and the true God, then the God of Masonry is *not* the true God. There is no escape from one of these two conclusions. Which conclusion is right is apparent to the merest novice.

Masonry has thousands of members who would never have entered it if they had to confess Jesus Christ as Lord and God to get in -- the Jewish members, for instance. But let Masonry speak for itself (p. 619):

"There is nothing in it (Masonry) to offend a Jew"!

Do you know what this means -- "There is nothing in Masonry to offend the Jew"? Let me tell you. Jesus Christ one day came to the Jews and said, "I and my Father are one." The Jews promptly picked up stones to stone Him. Jesus answered them, "Many good works have I showed you from my Father; for which of those works do ye stone me? The Jews answered him, saying, For a good work we stone thee not; but for *blasphemy;* and because that thou, being a man, makest thyself God" (John 10:30-33).

The Jews condemned Jesus Christ to death and delivered Him to the Romans for crucifixion because He claimed to be their own God, the mighty Jehovah! To this day the Jews regard Christianity as a blasphemous religion because we worship and confess Jesus Christ as Lord and God.

I tell you, if there is nothing in Masonry to offend

the Jew, then Masonry does not confess Jesus Christ as Lord and God, nor ask its initiates to do so. And if Masonry does not confess Jesus Christ, then Masonry does not confess the true God. And if Masonry does not confess the true God then Masonry confesses a false god. And if Masonry confesses a false god, let us be plain and call Masonry what it really is, by its own utterances, in the light of the Bible -- nothing but *paganism and idolatry!*

This is the exact teaching of the Bible. All worship and acknowledgment paid to any god apart from Jesus Christ is idolatry. "And we know that the Son of God is come, and hath given us an understanding, that we may know him that is true, and we are in him that is true, even in his Son Jesus Christ. *This is the true God,* and eternal life. Little children, keep yourselves from idols" (I John 5:20-21) . . .

But someone may say: "It is true that Jesus Christ is not confessed in the first three degrees, but He is confessed as God in some of the higher degrees of Masonry."

Well, I will have to take your word for it. This Masonic encyclopedia contains articles on almost every false god of the pagan world, but it contains not even the trace of an article on Jesus Christ, the Son of God. This is a significant and ominous omission.

But suppose it is true that Christ is recognized as God in some of the higher degrees, such as the Knights Templar. What of it? Does that clear the skirts of the organization? Let me ask you a question: "Can you reach those higher degrees, can you become a Knight Templar without passing through the first three degrees?" No; you cannot. That settles the question. Will any intelligent, enlightened Christian affirm that it is permissible to become an idolater first in order that afterward he may be a Christian? Will he affirm that it is right to first bow the knee at the altar of a false god in order that afterward he may bow the knee to the true God? Will Jesus Christ accept a confession of His deity from the mouth of man whose lips are defiled with the confession of a false god? How foolish.

Suppose a Buddhist should come to me and say: "We have an organization we would like you to join. In order to take the first three degrees, you will have to acknowledge a god, but not your Christ. Afterward, we will fix up a place in the organization and invent some new degrees where you Christians can get together and confess your Christ."

Suppose I should start an organization here in this church with secret work and several degrees. The first three degrees would eliminate the name of Jesus Christ and demand that every candidate confess a god named "G.A.O.T.U." We would accept Christians, Jews, Mohammedans, Buddhists. After they had passed the first three degrees, we would say: "Now, if you Christians want to get together and confess your Christ, go up in a room by yourselves. You Mohammedans do the same," etc. "But don't drag your peculiar views into these three degrees."

That's what Masonry does. What a pitiful sop to throw to our blessed Lord Jesus Christ. As a Christian, I spurn it.

But all this discussion is altogether unnecessary. The encyclopedia declares that:

> "The germ and nucleus of all Freemasonry is to be found in the three primitive degrees" (p. 753).

And only last week a Thirty-Second Degree Mason, a friend of mine, said to me: "When a man has taken the first three degrees, he is as much a Mason as he can ever be! All the higher degrees are merely additions, superfluous."

Oh, the insult of it! To exclude Jesus Christ from the main building of Masonry, the foundation and basis of Masonry, and then to offer Him a place in a side room along with Mohammed, Buddha, and the rest of "the thieves and robbers." Masonry had better left Him out altogether than to offer Him this crowning insult. Even if some of His professed followers seem to be strangely blind, Masonry ought to have known that Jesus Christ would accept no place at all unless it be the place of *preeminence.* Colossians 1:18 declares that "in all things" Christ must have the "the preeminence." Masonry refuses Him the place of preeminence, therefore Masonry is a Christless institution.

Masonry even goes so far as to mutilate the Word of God in order to exclude Jesus Christ. I have here another work by the author of the encyclopedia. It is called "The Masonic Ritualist." Don't get excited -- it is not "The Ritual." It doesn't contain any of the secrets. According to the author, it contains "all that may be lawfully taught in print of the degrees." It gives the prayers and Scriptures which are to be read in the opening and closing of the lodge. Every Scripture used is emptied of Jesus Christ, but there is a particularly glaring mutilation on Page 271. I shall give the quotation exactly as it appears in the "Ritualist" followed by the author's explanatory note:

> 'Charge to be Read at Opening of the Lodge'
>
> "Wherefore, brethren, lay aside all malice, and guile, and hypocrisies, and envies, and all evil speakings.
>
> 'If so be ye have tasted that the Lord is gracious, to whom coming as unto a living stone, disallowed indeed of men, but chosen of God, and precious; ye also as living stones be ye built up a spiritual house, an holy priesthood, to offer up sacrifices acceptable to God . . . .'
>
> "(The passages of Scripture here selected are peculiarly appropriate to this degree . . . . The passages are taken, with slight but necessary modifications, from the second chapter of the First Epistle of Peter . . .)."

You will note that Dr. Mackey says some "slight but necessary modifications" have been made in these Scriptures. What are these "modifications"? Let me read I Peter 2:5 from the Bible and you will see.

"Ye also, as lively stones, are built up a spiritual house, an holy priesthood, to offer up spiritual sacrifices, acceptable to God *by Jesus Christ.*"

Do you see it? The name of Christ is struck out by the profane hand of Masonry! And mark you, this is said to be a "slight modification"! And still further, it is said to be a "necessary modification"! Certainly it is *necessary,* because Masonry pretends to be able to approach God and offer service to Him without coming through Jesus Christ. There are in this "Masonic Ritualist" 28 prayers, and not one of them is offered in the name of Jesus Christ!

This is the insolent answer of Masonry to the ultimatum of Christ -- "No man cometh unto the Father, but by me" (John 14:6).

Now I am ready to classify Freemasonry in the light of its own utterances and statements of the Word of God.

Masonry admits that it confesses a god, but does not confess Jesus Christ. Let me read you one passage -- I John 4:3 ASV -- "Every spirit that confesseth not Jesus is not of God: and this is the spirit of the anti-christ, whereof ye have heard that it cometh; and now it is in the world already." These are not my words. These are the words of God. Do you dare, as a Christian, wear the emblem of such an organization?

IV. BEFORE ACCEPTING ANY CHRISTIAN AS A MEMBER, MASONRY DEMANDS THAT HE DISOBEY JESUS CHRIST.

Obedience to the Lord Jesus Christ is the first and supreme duty of every Christian. Christ said in John 14:15, "If ye love me, keep my commandments." And I John 2:3-4 declares: "And hereby we do know that we know him, if we keep his commandments. He that saith, I know him, and keepeth not his commandments, is a liar and the truth is not in him."

Now let me read you something that was commanded by the Lord Jesus in the most solemn manner. "Swear not at all; neither by heaven; for it is God's throne: nor by the earth; for it is his footstool: neither by Jerusalem; for it is the city of the great King" (Matt. 5:34-35). Our Lord considered this thing so tremendously important that He caused it to be written a second time in the Scripture (James 5:12). Nothing is more plain in the Bible. The Christian is commanded by the Lord to swear not at all by any oath. The Government of the United States recognizes this and makes provision for Christians who believe in following the precept of the Lord. No Christian is obliged to take a civil oath. He is permitted to make a simple affirmation.

Now suppose I come to the door of Masonry and knock for admittance. Almost the first thing demanded of me is disobedience to the Lord Jesus. Before I can enter I must swear "to conceal and never reveal" any of the secrets of Masonry -- things I yet know nothing about. It matters not that Christ has said, "Swear not at all." Masonry says, "You *must* swear." For the true Christian there is but one response: "It is better to obey God than man."

Practically every Mason admits frankly that the taking of oaths is necessary to become a member, but I have met one or two who denied it. They said: "It is not an oath. It is only an obligation." One wonders what to think when one Mason says, "It is an oath," and another says, "It is not an oath." Somebody is wrong. We shall let this Masonic encyclopedia settle the matter. On page 522 Dr. Mackey discusses the "obligation of Masonic secrecy." He says the opponents of Masonry have brought five charges against this Masonic obligation of secrecy.

(1) It is an oath.

(2) It is administered before the secrets are communicated.

(3) It is accompanied by certain superstitious ceremonies.

(4) It is attended by a penalty.

(5) It is considered by the Masons as paramount to the obligations of the law of the land.

Mackey says further: "In replying to these statements it is evident that the conscientious Mason labors under great disadvantage. He is at every step restrained by his honor from either the denial or admission of his adversaries in relation to the mysteries of the Craft." "But," he says, *"it may be granted, for the sake of argument, that every one of the first four charges is true."* The last charge, Mackey says, is indignantly denied! But the first four are true!

Thus it is that Masonry with impunity asks men to disobey Jesus Christ, but at the same time it insists sternly that all its own mandates shall be obeyed immediately and implicitly. Page 525:

> "The first duty of every Mason is to obey the mandate of the master" (not Christ, but the master of the Lodge). "This spirit of instant obedience and submission to authority constitutes the great safeguard of the institution . . . The order must be at once obeyed. Its character and its consequences may be matters of subsequent inquiry. The Masonic rule of obedience is like the nautical imperative, 'Obey orders, even if you break owners.'"

Jesus Christ is the Owner of the Christian and the Christian must obey Him, not the profane voice of Masonry.

V. MASONRY TEACHES ITS MEMBERS THAT THEY MAY REACH HEAVEN, LIFE, AND IMMORTALITY BY A WAY APART FROM JESUS CHRIST.

If the Word of God teaches anything, it teaches that apart from Jesus Christ no man will ever reach heaven, see life, or receive immortality.

"Jesus saith unto him, I am the way, the truth, and the life: no man cometh unto the Father, but by me" (John 14:6) . . .

Masonry ignores Jesus Christ as the True Way of Salvation. These Masonic books contain not the slightest hint which I can find that any Mason can be lost forever. But everywhere and always it is assumed that the Mason at death will enter the "temple not made with hands," receive eternal life, and enjoy immortality in the presence of God forever. It is assumed in the funeral ritual. It is assumed in the Masonic prayers. It is taught in Masonic symbolism. From the mass of testimony I choose one quotation. Among its other paraphernalia, Masonry has a ladder which is brought into the lodge for the work of initiation, so I was told by a Thirty-Second Degree Mason in good standing. On page 361 this encyclopedia gives the meaning of the ladder.

> This ladder is a "symbol of progress . . . its three principal rounds, representing Faith, Hope, and Charity, present us with the means of advancing from earth to heaven, from death to life, from the mortal to immortality. Hence, its foot is placed on the ground floor of the Lodge, which is typical of the world, and its top rests on the covering of the Lodge, which is symbolic of heaven."

This is the Masonic way into heaven. The initiate is to climb into heaven by the ladder of Faith, Hope, and Charity. You say, "This sounds all right." But is it all right? Masonry has appropriated three beautiful words from the Bible, but what does Masonry mean by these words? Fortunately we are not left in the dark. The encyclopedia devotes an article to each word used in Masonry. "Faith" is faith in God (the god of Masonry). "Hope" is the hope of immortality. "Charity" is that love which the Mason shows toward brother Masons and fellow men.

Will such faith, hope, and charity save the soul of any man? You know it will not. If a man has nothing more than faith in God (and remember that the god of Masonry is not the true God), nothing more than hope for immortality, nothing is more certain than that man will be lost. The devils believe in God and tremble! All men hope for immortality. Most men show some charity.

There is only one faith that can save -- that is faith

in the Lord Jesus Christ! There is only one hope that is sure -- that is hope in the Lord Jesus Christ! There is only one charity which is recognized by God and rewarded -- that is charity extended in the name of Jesus Christ!

The faith demanded by Masonry is not in Christ. The hope taught by Masonry is not in Christ. The charity inculcated by Masonry is not in the name of Christ. The ladder of Masonry is not the Way of Jesus Christ. The fact of the matter is that a man does not need a ladder to get into heaven. Praise the Lord. The entrance to heaven is not by a ladder. It is by a *Door!*

Jesus said: "I am the door: by me if any man enter in, he shall be saved." Now listen: "He that entereth not by the door . . . but *climbeth up* some other way (mark the words), the same is a thief and a robber"! (John 10:1-9). Any organization which ignores the Lord Jesus Christ as the Door of heaven, and puts up a ladder of its own, is a thief and a robber. Christ said that!

The way of Masonry is not the Way of the Cross. It is the way of human works and human character.

Speaking of the "working tools" of the "Entered Apprentice" Mackey says:

> "THE COMMON GAVEL is an instrument made use of by operative masons to break off the corners of rough stones, the better to fit them for the builder's use; but we, as Free and Accepted Masons, are taught to make use of it for the more noble and glorious purpose of divesting our hearts and consciences of all the vices and superfluities of life; thereby fitting our minds as living stones for that spiritual building, that 'house not made with hands' eternal in the heavens" (The Ritualist, p. 39).

Oh, my friends, let me tell you upon the authority of God's Word that you can never get rid of your sins and vices with the "common gavel" of Masonry. You can never fit yourself for "the house not made with hands, eternal in the heavens." There is just one thing that can take away sins and make you fit to enter the blessed house -- *the blood of Jesus Christ!* "Unto him that loved us, and washed us from our sins in his own blood . . . to him be glory and dominion for ever and ever. Amen" (Rev. 1:5-6).

You say: "If Masonry is such a terrible institution, why don't other men condemn it?" They do. John Adams condemned it. Also John Quincy Adams, James Madison, Millard Fillmore, Daniel Webster, Charles Sumner. Of the great evangelists, Finney condemned it. Moody condemned it. Torrey said: "I do not believe it is possible for a man to be an intelligent Christian and an intelligent Mason at the same time." George F. Pentecost, late pastor of the Wanamaker Church in this city, said: "I believe that Masonry is an incalculable evil and essentially antichrist in its principles and influences." He should have known something about it, for a Thirty-Second Degree Mason told me last week that church had a lodge within its own membership.

Why do Christian men stay in it? I can think of only four reasons why you find professing Christians affiliated with the Masonic lodge:

First -- Some do not know what Christianity really is. Many have the prevalent but erroneous opinion that Christianity and religion are one and the same thing. If an organization is religious and talks about God, they conclude it is Christian. Such people are sincere but untaught. Because they do not know what Christianity is, they see nothing wrong with Masonry. These deserve our sympathy. If there is to be any blame, it belongs to the pastors who have failed to teach them the truth.

Second -- Some do not know what Masonry really is. It is possible that some here may scoff at the idea of a Mason not knowing what his lodge stands for. Nevertheless, it is true that there are thousands of Masons who are not acquainted with the religious position of Masonry as an institution. I have met

Thirty-Second Degree Masons who frankly admitted that they had never read even one Masonic authority such as this encyclopedia. Within the past month I have actually found Masons who even denied the existence of such works. Yet the Masonic Temple of this city has a fair-sized library of books on Masonry, many of which are accessible to the non-Masonic public.

You may think that such ignorance is impossible. Not at all. You find it in every organization. I think I could find members of the Brethren Church here at this place who have never read a book setting forth the position of the denomination and who would be unable to state it. It is the same in every church whether Presbyterian, Methodist, or Baptist. If such ignorance can be found in organizations where public instruction is given several times each week, it is not surprising to find it in Masonry. The average Mason is like some church members. He only does what is absolutely necessary to become a member and stops there. His knowledge of Masonry is based upon his little experience in a local lodge and he never makes any effort to ascertain exactly what is the religious position of Masonry as a great institution.

Permit me to say in all kindness, that the gentleman who rose at the beginning of this sermon to protest against the charge that Masonry is not Christian, is an illustration of what I am saying. He has admitted before you all, in an answer to my question, that *he has never read even one Masonic authority.* We have no denunciation for such men, but in the name of Jesus Christ we beg that they will investigate the institution to which they are giving their allegiance.

Third -- A few professing Christians continue their relation with Masonry in spite of the fact that they know what Christianity is, and also what Masonry is. Such as these are without excuse. They are living every day in deliberate disloyalty to the Lord Jesus Christ, who died for their sins. They deserve blame, not sympathy.

Fourth -- There are some professing Christians in Masonry who are apostate from the true faith. Some of the preachers in Masonry belong in this classification. They have relegated such truths as Blood Atonement and the Deity of Christ to the place of nonessentials. They are virtually Unitarian in belief, and therefore it is not surprising to find them in an institution which in its three main degrees is Unitarianism, so much so that ex-President Taft, a prominent Unitarian, feels at home in it. The presence of such men in Masonry is an argument against it, not for it.

"But," you say, "there are good men in it. Washington was a Mason." Yes; and Washington was a slave-owner also. You are not to follow men. If you follow men you are heading for disaster. Christ says to the Christian, "Follow thou me."

I must close, though I have only begun. This encyclopedia contains enough that is anti-Christian to keep me preaching for the next ten weeks every Sunday night. I have said enough to condemn this institution forever in the eyes of you who know Jesus Christ and love Him. I have tried not to be harsh or unkind. I have tried to tell you the truth. Jesus Christ is the only hope for men. My only motive tonight has been to get you to be loyal to Him.

A man says: "It will hurt me if I leave Masonry now." I know it will. But oh, Christian, did your Christ fail you at the cross because it hurt? By the blood of His cross I plead with you: "Come out from among them, and be ye separate." "Be not unequally yoked together with unbelievers: for what fellowship hath righteousness with unrighteousness? and what communion hath light with darkness? And what concord hath Christ with Belial? or what part hath he that believeth with an infidel? And what agreement hath the temple of God with idols?" (II Cor. 6:14-17).

"Mick" McClain hadn't lost his ability to throw the forward pass. Only 10 years earlier he would have relied on his wit, on his practiced eye, and on deception to slip by the opposing team; now he was able to rely on the Spirit of God, on His Word, and on the sledgehammer blows of truth which needed only to be presented. The Philadelphia sermon caused a stir and was later published in a pamphlet which followed him to the end, supporting his case and bringing enlightenment or anger, deliverance or contempt from all who read it.

For the bulletin board in front of the Philadelphia church Pastor McClain wrote catchy phrases and mind-probing maxims about God, the Bible, human history, and faith. People walking by, riding street cars or traveling by automobile came to enjoy the messages of the bulletin board. Many came into the church because of them.

One was Alice Longaker who later joined the church. She discovered that her pastor was typing his own letters, filing, and generally carrying out alone the secretarial duties on matters relating to the Foreign Missionary Board. She offered to take dictation in the evening and type his letters on her own typewriter at home. Alice later settled in Long Beach, California, and became a secretary to L. S. Bauman.

In Philadelphia, Pastor McClain wrote for the *Sunday School Times* unsigned editorials on a variety of subjects. In Pittsburgh, one Sunday, he preached a sermon which he had written for one of those editorials. Afterward someone in the audience came up and charged him with plagiarism. "I read your exact message," he said, "in the *Sunday School Times*, and that's where I think you got it."

In Philadelphia, Alva J. McClain wrote a historic document that will be cited later. It became the touchstone for conservatism in the denomination's tug of war a decade later. Titled, "The Message of the Brethren Ministry," it was adopted as the church's official statement of faith in its 1921 National Conference.

From 1919 to 1923 he taught apologetics in night

classes at the Philadelphia School of the Bible, 1921-25 Spring Garden Street -- a school founded by Drs. William Pettingill and C. I. Scofield in 1914. Many in McClain's night classes were professional people and many later joined his church. One was an alert young man with piercing eyes and dark black hair named Orville D. Jobson. This man became fast friends with his teacher and later went to the Central African Republic as a missionary with the Brethren Church.

Five years passed in Philadelphia. Pastor McClain was becoming more and more eager to obtain the elusive liberal arts degree which he had missed in other schooling. In 1923, he resigned and moved back to L.A. where he enrolled in Occidental College and finished in 1925 with highest honor. He studied at Occidental under the direction of the faculty at Xenia Theological Seminary to complete work for his Master of Theology degree and wrote his dissertation at Occidental. Upon graduation he received Phi Beta Kappa recognition retroactive for 15 years. From 1925 until his death, he was rarely seen in full dress without his Phi Beta Kappa key. The administration at Xenia wanted him to appear in graduation exercises to receive his Th.M. degree after he received also his Bachelor of Arts degree, but Occidental would not excuse him from giving his valedictorian address.

The youthful scholar was in constant demand for preaching missions at Bible conferences inside his denomination and out. He spoke at the Moody Bible Institute's annual Bible conferences, at Canadian Keswick Conferences, at the large Bible and Missionary Conference of Calvary Independent Church in Lancaster, Pennsylvania and in churches from one end of the country to the other. He was once scheduled to travel to mission fields of Africa, teaching Bible classes on the ship en route, but he became ill at the departure time and was not able to travel. This had been the only trip ever planned beyond the shores of the United States. Dr. McClain delivered the Bueer-mann Memorial Lectures at the Western Conservative Baptist Seminary in Portland, Oregon and spoke often at Dallas Theological Seminary, having been invited to serve on its faculty when the school was started by Lewis Sperry Schafer.

6

'J' Accuse'

Throughout his education and pastoral experience Alva J. McClain watched the encroachment of liberalism within Ashland College, and particularly in the Bible department loosely referred to as the "seminary" after 1906. Brethren ministerial students spent four years in the college majoring in Theology and Bible, then received the Bachelor of Arts degree at graduation. In later years, this degree was changed to the "A.B. in Divinity" to more clearly represent the studies undertaken.

Because The Brethren Church had no full-fledged seminary, many of the young men within the church went to universities and theological schools outside their own denomination where they came in contact with liberal theological views. One such individual was

Dr. J. L. Gillin who took advanced studies at Columbia University and Union Theological Seminary. Dr. Gillin was named president of Ashland College in which position he served from 1906 to 1911. Because of his elite education and abilities, he became a leader in the liberal movement which was creeping steadily throughout the church.

Dr. McClain took careful notes during national conferences as the various representatives of Ashland College spoke. At the 1914 conference he heard Dr. Gillin seriously propose that "religious experience" might be substituted for an "infallible Bible" as the true basis of Christian authority.

At the 1915 conference Dr. Gillin went further. He minimized the importance of the deity of Christ by saying, "A person may be a member of the Brethren . . . and be an Athanasian on the subject of the nature of Christ (a reference to the views of Athanasius, bishop of Alexandria who wrote an ecumenical creed) or on the other hand he may be an Arian (one who holds the view that God created Christ and so came into being after God) and still be a good member of the church. These things are of minor importance."

Such remarks by Dr. Gillin began to draw the lines more clearly between the liberals and the conservatives within the denomination. L. S. Bauman took the lead of a passionate but unorganized opposition. His files from 1915 through to 1921 are filled with correspondence between pastors, students, teachers, and administrative heads at Ashland College. To the liberals' dismay, the dean of Ashland's "seminary", Dr. J. Allen Miller, stood firmly on the side of the conservatives.

By 1921, the National Conference was prepared to adopt by an overwhelming majority the document previously cited titled, "The Message of the Brethren Ministry." This document provided the rallying point around which the evangelical Brethren gathered. It has appeared often in Brethren literature just as Pastor McClain wrote it in 1921:

THE MESSAGE OF THE BRETHREN MINISTRY

The Message which Brethren Ministers accept as a divine entrustment to be heralded to a lost world, finds its sole source and authority in the Bible. This message is one of hope for a lost world and speaks with finality and authority. Fidelity to the apostolic injunction to preach the Word demands our utmost endeavor of mind and heart. We, the members of the National Ministerial Association of The Brethren Church, hold that the essential and constituent elements of our message shall continue to be the following declarations:

1. Our motto:

The Bible, the whole Bible and nothing but the Bible.

2. The authority and integrity of the Holy Scriptures.

The ministry of The Brethren Church desires to bear testimony to the belief that God's supreme revelation has been made through Jesus Christ, a complete and authentic record of which revelation is the New Testament; and, to the belief that the Holy Scripture of the Old and New Testaments, as originally given, are the infallible record of the perfect, final and authoritative revelation of God's will, altogether sufficient in themselves as a rule of faith and practice.

3. We understand the basic content of our doctrinal preaching to be:

(1) The Pre-Existence, Deity and Incarnation by Virgin Birth of Jesus Christ, the Son of God;

(2) The Fall of Man, his consequent spiritual death and utter sinfulness, and the necessity of his New Birth;

(3) The Vicarious Atonement of the Lord Jesus Christ through the shedding of His own blood;

(4) The Resurrection of the Lord Jesus Christ in the body in which He suffered and died, and His subsequent glorification at the right hand of God;

(5) Justification by personal faith in the Lord Jesus Christ, of which obedience to the will of God, and works of righteousness, are the evidence and

result; the resurrection of the dead, the judgment of the world, and the life everlasting of the just;

(6) The Personality and Deity of the Holy Spirit, Who indwells the Christian and is his Comforter and Guide;

(7) The personal and visible return of our Lord Jesus Christ from heaven as King of kings and Lord of lords, the glorious goal for which we are taught to watch, wait and pray;

(8) The Christian should "be not conformed to this world, but be transformed by the renewing of the mind", should not engage in carnal strife, and should "swear not at all";

(9) The Christian should observe, as his duty and privilege, the ordinances of our Lord Jesus Christ, among which are: (a) Baptism of Believers by Trine Immersion; (b) Confirmation; (c) the Lord's Supper; (d) the Communion of the Bread and Wine; (e) the Washing of the Saints' Feet; and (f) the Anointing of the Sick with Oil.

With a few deft strokes which grew out of a head full of truth and a heart full of loyalty, the denomination's young pastor had rallied the evangelicals, stopped Dr. Gillin from attending National Conference, and given the churches a larger voice in Ashland College's faculty selections.

The whirlwind drew in McClain himself. Dean J. Allen Miller, enthusiastic for the "Message of the Brethren Ministry," asked Dr. McClain to join the "seminary" faculty, to organize a graduate school of theology, to prepare a commensurate curriculum, and to write a catalog. In 1925 McClain accepted, becoming Professor of Theology and Apologetics at Ashland while serving as Associate Dean.

Professor McClain didn't get far with his program. After two years, he saw clearly that the prospects for establishing on campus a bona fide theological seminary on a graduate level were dim. Students interested in becoming ministers were switching to the bachelor of arts program so they would be qualified to enter graduate-level theological training afterward.

Clearly the college administration was not in sympathy with its theological program. Discontentment surfaced in board meetings of the trustees and cropped out in practical ways on campus. William H. Schaffer, a pastor in Conemaugh, Pennsylvania, with a distinguished ministry there, recalls the high scorn of collegians when seminary boys began handing out tracts on campus.

The frail health that plagued the man from Sunnyside plus the opposition by liberals on campus, led to his resignation after two years in Ashland. President Edwin E. Jacobs tried to persuade him to stay, but at the close of school in 1927, Alva and Jo steered their Packard westward and took up residence in Hollywood. From 1927 to 1929 he taught Christian Doctrine at The Bible Institute of Los Angeles. He continued to work on a program and curriculum, looking toward the eventual establishment of a theological seminary which would embody certain educational objectives and ideals which he felt were not being fully realized in any existing school. McClain couldn't see why a school could not enjoy the warm intimacy of a Bible college while at the same time offering the highest academic accreditation and theological conservatism possible.

"I wanted," he once wrote, "a school where the competent scholarship of a seminary might function within the warm spiritual and practical atmosphere of a Bible institute."

His mentor, L. S. Bauman, was the logical ally. Bauman, like Peter, was always ready to take action. At that moment, his church was building a large educational wing in Long Beach, "the perfect place for your seminary." Bauman hired McClain to serve as Minister of Education while plans for the new seminary were being formulated. Local friends and members of the Brethren Church from sea to sea heard of the project and promised their support.

Prominent laymen in the Long Beach church also promised financial help. Prospective students were registering informally even before the building was completed.

Word of the new project filtered down to President Jacobs at Ashland College. Presidents of church schools take special note when members begin to run competition and drain off funds which might otherwise have come to the official denominational institution. On July 3, 1929, President Jacobs wrote to Pastor Bauman:

> I note what you say about the seminary on the [west] coast. Naturally I would rather not see it there . . . I am inclined to think in time the seminary there would militate against the work here . . . I would be much better pleased, and I think the church would be better served, if a way were provided to bring McClain here and the seminary. His very presence here . . . would mean a world of good to us. I have absolute confidence in him and in his ability to enthuse our young men as they ought to be enthused.

After the letter had time to circulate among all parties concerned, the school sent out a representative in the person of Dr. W. S. Bell, the Sunnyside pastor who had baptized Alva McClain in 1912. Dr. Bell was at that time endowment secretary at Ashland College. His department had the most to lose by the divided allegiance of the Brethren. With the conviction of a salesman he expressed his strong feeling that the new seminary should be launched in organic relation with the college at Ashland College. It would be welcomed there, he assured the men, and urged that its influence on campus would do much to keep the college true to the faith.

"I urge both you men, Dr. Bauman and Dr. McClain, to attend the April meeting of the board of trustees," said Dr. Bell. "In fact," he added, "if you don't, the California school will attract the major interest and support of the churches and might result eventually in the loss of the college."

United, he reasoned, the Brethren could keep seminary and college; divided they might lose both.

"The college should assume the financial support for the school if placed at Ashland," Dr. Bell stated.

The emissary took the train for home, satisfied that his mission had been accomplished. He wrote on March 4, 1930:

> Dear Dr. McClain:
>
> It has been decided to have our college board of trustees meet on April 22. I hope you and Bauman can be here as it will be very important that you should, at least one of you. I am satisfied that the two institutions (seminary and college) cannot be maintained separately at the present time without the loss of the college.

The two Californians agreed to meet with the college board at Ashland to explore possibilities. They wanted, after all, not to jeopardize the future either of the college or of the proposed new seminary. The two were not outsiders. Dr. Bauman was already a member of the Ashland College board, representing the churches of the strong Southern California District. Professor McClain had been elected moderator of the General Conference of the Brethren Church for the current year of 1929-30.

At the annual meeting of the board, McClain presented his plan, dealing methodically with three things:

"First, the need for a standard Brethren theological seminary; second, the reasons why the Ashland College campus would *not* be the best to locate it; and third, some essential conditions which must be met if the seminary were to be located there."

Excerpts from the McClain report:

> The Brethren Church must provide theological training for its own ministry. If we do not, our best young men will go elsewhere. Some have already made application to enter other seminaries . . . The Brethren Church cannot depend upon the arts college at Ashland to do this work. By its very nature

the arts college must either be silent or else keep in the background the distinctive positions of the Brethren Church . . . . We need a theological seminary which, by example and precept, will lead men to feel that it is supremely worthwhile to be a minister *in the Brethren Church* . . . . Without an adequately trained ministry, enthusiastic for our message, we are doomed. Competition is keen, union is in the air, and modernism is dissolving all differences."

With regard to the location of the seminary, Professor McClain argued that while there would be some advantages in placing it at Ashland College, there were other reasons which could be argued against such a location. He continued:

The Seminary should be conducted in a religious atmosphere which does not and cannot possibly exist in an arts college which is open to the general public and where the seminary students are a small minority . . . . It should be frankly recognized that the [Ashland] college faculty contains an element which does not sympathize with the theological viewpoint of the seminary and a majority of Brethren ministers. The seminary professors should not be handicapped by the unpleasant task of correcting erroneous theological opinions expressed in [college] classroom and chapel. It is not that such opinions are feared. But it is demoralizing and embarrassing to have these issues arising between faculty members of the same institution . . . . If the seminary teacher ventures to defend the church's viewpoint, he is likely to be regarded as a troublesome heresy hunter and placed in a false light before the [college] student body. If the arts college would support enthusiastically the theological position of the seminary, this situation could be corrected. But experience does not indicate much hope for such a solution, although it might properly be expected of a church college . . . . In some respects, the presence of the seminary on the Ashland campus would be an embarrassment to the arts college. Such seminary work as we are doing there at present is being done surreptitiously. To borrow a well-understood term, we are "bootlegging" our seminary education as far as graduate work is concerned. This will be perfectly clear to anyone who reads the college catalog (1930) . . . . The situation is demoralizing to the best interests of ministerial training in the Brethren Church . . . . If the college [administration] demands the retention of the seminary on this campus, it should be given the dignity and prestige that such a school deserves and must have.

In concluding his presentation of the new seminary project, Professor McClain assured the board that although the men for whom he spoke were strongly in favor of locating the school in Southern California where both a building and financial support were available, nevertheless they might agree to the location at Ashland College if the board would approve and support a definite *"seminary program"* which he then proceeded to outline.

The historic document is presented as Alva J. McClain wrote it originally:

1. The present seminary department of the arts college should be made a standard theological seminary for college graduates . . . degrees to be granted only to those who have properly matriculated.

2. The faculty shall be composed of at least four professors . . .

3. The dean of the seminary should have complete jurisdiction in all seminary matters, similar to the jurisdiction of the president in the arts college . . . . He should be a member of the board of trustees in order that the seminary interests may be properly represented thereon.

4. Teachers having the degree of Th.M. from standard seminaries should be ranked with the doctors in the arts college, in such matters as scholastic standing and salary . . . . (If the two institutions were separated, this issue would not be raised.)

5. The continuance of the seminary on the college grounds should be regarded as an experiment for the

present, and if it proves successful, steps shall be taken to erect a separate building suited to the special needs of the seminary. On the other hand, if the separation of the two institutions should be finally deemed advisable, both college and seminary shall cooperate in the matter so that it may be accomplished without injury to either.

6. A plan should be worked out which will insure the financial autonomy of the seminary. This plan should provide either for an equitable division of present and future endowment income between college and seminary, or else authorize the seminary to conduct its own campaign for endowment.

7. The seminary should publish its own annual catalog and bulletin.

8. Within the board of trustees, there should be a seminary committee composed of at least five members appointed by the president of the board in consultation with the seminary faculty. The dean of the seminary should be a member ex officio of this committee.

Like the Israelite milch kine, with their calves tied up at home [see I Samuel 6:10] the board dragged McClain's "ark" back to campus, lowing as they went. They had acquiesced without approving. Their unhappiness was clear to all who heard them vote their "ayes," but the matter passed. Years later, Professor McClain could gamely understand their reluctance. The college a month earlier had at last secured academic accreditation from the North Central Association. The added expense of the new seminary plan would to that extent reduce the funds available and much needed in the college to maintain the accrediting standards. The establishment of the seminary as a *graduate* school, they reasoned, might injure the academic position of the college in the eyes of the North Central examiners who were not interested in positive Christian theological education. It was an open secret that some college faculty members would have been only too glad to get rid of the seminary entirely.

There was still another reason for the "lowing." A college endowment campaign was in progress among the churches, and the most potent argument being used to secure financial support from the churches was that Ashland College provided education for the ministers and missionaries of the church. Therefore, the administration hesitated to consent to the establishment of the seminary elsewhere since it would attract the financial support of the churches, most of which were more interested in training students for full-time Christian service than in merely supplementing the secular educational facilities already existing in half a hundred other institutions in the State of Ohio. How could the disgruntled object? They did not welcome the prospect of its coming there, but to have it go elsewhere appeared to be worse. So, the decision was made.

A faculty persuaded against its will is of the same opinion still.

Supporters argued convincingly that the central location of Ohio made the new graduate school more easily available to all the churches of the denomination. McClain was in the driver's seat. Deep down, he knew that the optimistic views were whistles in the dark, yet he was prepared to give the new school every ounce of his professional wisdom, experience, and theological expertise.

The Brethren Evangelist magazine kept the church apprised editorially. In the May 3, 1930 issue President Jacobs publically announced certain actions which had been taken at the recent college board meeting. Among other things, he wrote:

> With the seminary here along with the arts college, our interests will not be divided. There will be no question about the granting of suitable degrees, and everything points to the wisdom of such a choice. More will be said about the situation at length later through these columns.

In the Educational issue of the *Evangelist,* May 31,

1930, Rev. George T. Ronk, president of the college board, announced formally:

At the recent meeting of the board of trustees arrangements were made for establishment of a postgraduate seminary with power to grant graduate degrees in three-year and four-year courses in theological training . . . . Beginning with the first of next September, all new students for the seminary in full-course work must enter the college of liberal arts and graduate therefrom before admittance into the seminary.

In the same issue of the *Evangelist* Professor McClain presented an extensive outline of the recently adopted "New Seminary Program," under which:

The present seminary department of the college will be enlarged and advanced to the rank of a standard theological seminary for college graduates . . . . All the seminary courses are to be revised and raised to the level of graduate work . . . . The emphasis of the school will be fourfold: orthodox belief, spiritual living, thorough scholarship, and practical application."

As executive head of the new school, Professor McClain announced that the departments and teachers would be arranged as follows:

Dr. J. Allen Miller, dean; department of New Testament and Greek, with an adjunct in Philosophy.

Prof. Alva J. McClain, associate dean: Department of Theology and Christian Evidences, with an adjunct in English Bible.

Prof. Melvin A. Stuckey: Department of Homiletics and Practical Theology, with an adjunct in Church History.

Prof. Kenneth M. Monroe: Department of Old Testament and Hebrew, with an adjunct in Archeology.

At the 1930 National Conference on August 26, it was time again to report. Like a coach with a winning team, Professor McClain told his brothers and sisters:

This fall for the first time in the history of the Brethren Church we shall be able to offer our young men a regular three years' seminary course for college graduates . . . . It seems to me, therefore, that this General Conference should take cognizance of the situation and recommend to the various districts and congregations a wholehearted support of the seminary program.

The Conference, by formal action, approved the recommended plan.

Professor and Mrs. McClain moved into the second half of a duplex owned and occupied by Dean J. Allen Miller directly across the street from the campus. He outlined the first seminary catalog and wrote much of its material. It carried as a statement of Christian faith the document he wrote for the National Conference of 1921. "The Message of the Brethren Ministry," adopted by the Brethren National Ministerial Association.

By 1932, seminary enrollment stood at 18. Steady streams of preseminary students were moving up through the college. The seminary faculty felt obliged to counsel these upcoming enrollees to help them maintain their Christian convictions -- convictions that were not important to many college faculty members. In joint chapel sessions, opposing religious viewpoints were often expressed. Students were quick to sense these conflicting views and to take sides according to their inclinations.

Professor McClain's annual report to the board of trustees on April 25, 1933, was blunt:

> Since the church commits its ministerial students to the college for a period of four years, a very grave responsibility rests upon the college teachers. Upon their personal attitudes will depend largely whether or not the student comes to the seminary with his life purpose intact or seriously damaged . . . . I think the board should give some serious consideration to this matter. I have tried to present it as generally as possible.

The hour was late; members were tired; a compromise was accepted. It seemed at the moment to be a great victory. At last the college had a definite standard of faith. This proved to be, however, merely the beginning of the battle. The seminary faculty adopted the new statement at once and published it prominently in the seminary catalog. Later the college faculty, in an atmosphere of restrained hostility, adopted the statement with a few scattered "ayes." Most did not vote. They were merely allowing the administration to honor its pledge to the board. The president made copies and mailed them to the ministers of the church, but he refused to publish the statement in the college catalog. There was never any serious effort to apply these standards of faith to any individual member of the college faculty.

At the same board meeting in 1933, Dr. J. Allen Miller became dean emeritus and Professor McClain was made the dean of the seminary.

By 1934 the problems of the college were dramatic. The accrediting agency removed Ashland College from its list of accredited institutions. The confidence of many pastors in the school had been shaken by the administration's failure to apply the standards of faith. Collegians were discontent; many preseminary students were being disturbed by anti-Biblical attitudes in certain classrooms; teachers Professor McClain called "the worldly majority" were clamoring for greater liberty than that allowed by the somewhat feeble rules.

Tension increased between seminary and college. It was heightened when the president suddenly stopped three seminary professors from teaching Bible classes in the college, and also ruled that no college credit would be given for Bible courses taken by college students in the seminary classes. Certain prominent college teachers began to agitate for a change of administration.

At the spring meeting of 1935, the board of trustees accepted the resignation of President Jacobs and elected to that position Dr. Charles L. Anspach, a former dean of the college. The death of Dr. J. Allen Miller had left vacant the professorship of New Testament and Greek in the seminary. To this position the board called Herman A. Hoyt, a brilliant linguistic student and protege of his former teacher.

Dean McClain had reason to believe that President Anspach's administration was the promise of a new day. For many hours, the new president consulted personally with the seminary dean about the course of the future. Dr. Anspach pledged to adhere to the college standards of faith. He said he would publish them in the college catalog and "stand by them."

"I have decided," President Anspach wrote to Dean McClain on February 11, 1935, "to accept the presidency."

What about the liberalism on campus?

"I admit there has been wrong teaching going on here, but my policy is to reorganize with the Wheaton [College] viewpoint and contact conservative men in all denominations. In this direction there is hope, while there is none in the direction of liberalism."

The letter was clear and comforting. There was no misunderstanding Dr. Anspach. Furthermore, at a meeting of representatives of both seminary and college, the new president announced his program and then asked each professor present whether he would agree to cooperate in his program.

The seminary teachers readily agreed, for it was their program. The college contingent acquiesced reluctantly. They were not able to make promises as easily as the new president, but nevertheless, the conservatives hoped for a better day.

Dean McClain's report in 1935 to the college board referred to conditions in part as follows:

> The baneful influence of fraternities . . . faculty worldliness, including addiction to cigarettes, cards, and movies . . . tolerance toward smoking and dancing by the students . . . drinking and public drunkenness among students, with no apparent serious at-

tempts to investigate thoroughly and discipline . . . contemptuous attitude toward the church and its ministry . . . questioning the truths of Christianity, and the teaching of the dogma of evolution . . . denunciation of the seminary as being responsible for the difficulties here . . . attempts to discredit the character of the seminary work by claiming to students that it had "no academic value" . . . spreading reports throughout the community that the seminary teachers are troublemakers . . . . These charges can be verified if the board wishes to investigate . . . . We believe the coming of Dr. Anspach will begin immediately to change these conditions under which we have had to work. His program for the institution, as outlined by him upon several occasions, is the program we have believed in and prayed for through the years . . . . Every difficulty that has ever arisen between seminary and college administration has had to do, either directly or indirectly, with Christian faith and life. No other problem exists. Our battle is not over men, but over truth. We do not hate men; we do hate untruth and error. And we do not propose to surrender when it arises. If you expect us to, do not ask us to remain here. We believe that, if Dr. Anspach's program is loyally and enthusiastically supported, this institution can become, by God's grace, one of the most outstanding educational institutions in America, spiritually and intellectually.

The man who took the presidency with the strongest support of any man within memory at Ashland College began in a few months to disappoint those who had backed him so enthusiastically. Solemn vows were forgotten, leading the church into a division which created two national conferences. Dean McClain, looking back, was convinced that the existing differences could have been handled without such far-reaching results if the actions of Dr. Anspach had been "tempered with more wisdom and good will."

Professor McClain listed the following actions to prove his charges:

A clear indication of his real inclinations appeared when the new president became sharply critical of the seminary because its teachers protested the inclusion of certain religious modernists on his inaugural program . . . .

One of his first administrative acts was the proposal of certain constitutional changes to permit a substantial increase of non-Brethren membership on the board, and depriving the church districts of their former elective powers, thus making the board self-perpetuating. This was serious enough for the College, but far worse for the seminary which was controlled by the same board.

Again, he began to reduce arbitrarily the small financial allowance made to the seminary for essential activities such as the annual day of prayer. In his first year it was found that, in spite of his former pledges, the new president was actually sympathetic with the very teachers in the college whose attitudes had caused much of the difficulty under the former administration.

During the academic year of 1935-36, Dr. Kenneth M. Monroe resigned his position as professor of the Old Testament, and President Anspach authorized Dean McClain to secure for this position Rev. Homer A. Kent, Sr., then pastor of the First Brethren Church of Washington, D.C. After the pastor had accepted the call, Dr. Anspach suddenly reversed himself, to the great embarrassment of all concerned, leaving the seminary with less than the minimum number of teachers necessary to maintain standard theological work.

At the 1936 meeting of the board, a large part of the president's report was devoted to what Dean McClain considered to be "an unwarranted and rather petty" attack upon the group of preseminary college students mentioned earlier who had distributed Christian tracts on the campus. President Anspach submitted a plan to divide the college student body into two groups in relation to "standards of living and conduct"; the one group would be permitted to uphold "restricted standards"; the other and larger group would not be required to live in harmony with such restricted standards of "social activities"; and the view of each group were to be "respected and protected."

Dean McClain called the proposal "absurd," but it was supported by a majority of board members present. It aroused widespread indignation, provoked the resignation of Dr. L. S. Bauman from the board, and subsequently resulted in the "Open Letter" addressed to the president of Ashland College by the Brethren Ministerial Board of the Southern California District.

Before the historic disconnection was to transpire, Ashland College and Alva J. McClain had many miles yet to go in 1936. After the professor's "Open Letter" had been distributed throughout the churches, President Anspach worked harder to defend his actions and to rally support for his administration.

When the 1936 National Conference convened in August, the main issues had become clear to the Brethren. First, the protection of "liberalism" in the college because of the refusal of the administration to apply the officially adopted standards of faith; second, the question of church control over its board; third, the conflict over standards of life and conduct on the campus; fourth, concern regarding the future of the seminary under the jurisdiction of a president hostile to a large segment of the church, a president who had the majority support on his board.

The "Ashland Problem" reached the floor early in the General Conference where it was discussed to some extent. The delegates passed the following actions in 1936 to attempt to solve the problem:

First, after the original charter of Ashland College was read from the podium, a motion was made that the Conference appoint a committee of seven men to investigate the condition causing the disturbance and report back to the General Conference in 1937. The motion passed with a fair majority. On that committee were R. D. Barnard, C. A. Stewart, R. F. Porte, William Schaffer Jr., Roy Patterson, E. H. Wolfe, and H. V. Wall. The college informed the committee it would have to wait for an invitation from the board which would not meet until the following spring.

Second, as to the proposal of the college president to increase the non-Brethren membership on the board, the General Conference adopted a strongly worded resolution warning of the danger of opening the door to modernistic control, and disapproving his proposal. Again the college administration fought the Conference action, and subsequently proceeded to carry out what the conference had disapproved.

Third, hurting from the drift of the Conference action, friends of Dr. Anspach proposed a motion of confidence in him and the entire administration of Ashland College. This motion was tabled by the Conference.

Back in Ashland, Charles Anspach proceeded to make things uncomfortable for those seminary teachers who continued to insist on the use of the college Statement of Faith. The climax came early in 1937 when the entire faculty of the institution met to consider a proposed code of "Rules and Regulations" for their organization and guidance. This code provided, among other things, that "a member of the teaching staff may be dismissed . . . for inefficiency or neglect of academic duty, immorality, or conduct unbecoming a gentleman." Dean McClain moved the addition of another cause for dismissal, namely, "for teaching anything contrary to the college Statement of Faith." This motion was quickly defeated by a loud chorus of "No's." Pointing out the seriousness of this action, Dean McClain asked that his own affirmative vote be made a matter of record. Professor Herman A. Hoyt made the same request. Someone moved that *all* the votes be so recorded, but the motion was overwhelmingly defeated.

Dr. L. L. Garber at this point informed the chairman that anyone could demand a roll-call vote by parliamentary procedure. Instantly, Professor Hoyt made the demand, and the roll-call began. It happened so quickly that the opposition had no time to collect its wits, and the chairman simply moved with the tide. Otherwise, the issue might never have come to a clean-cut public decision, as it did, with no escape for anyone.

"Charles Anspach" was the second name called in the alphabetical order of voting. He made an angry speech against the application of the college Statement of Faith and voted an emphatic "No," after which there was no longer any uncertainty as to the safe way to vote. When the tally was finished, only five votes were recorded as favoring the application of the Statement of Faith. Three of the votes were cast by the seminary teachers -- McClain, Hoyt, and Stuckey. Only two college teachers supported the seminary position -- Dr. Garber and Dr. Scholl.

The action just described brought an end to the theological seminary which stood for uncompromising loyalty to the Statement of Faith. To head off the fateful decision, Dean McClain made a final and friendly appeal to Dr. Anspach not to "act recklessly" because of the wide area of church interests which were involved. The appeal was fruitless. The administration was already busily engaged in assembling to its support various small groups which had little in common except a feeling of resentment against the determined stand of the seminary for the application of the college Statement of Faith.

When the board met at Ashland on June 1, 1937, with Bill Schaffer sitting in a corner at the back of the room to take notes for the Committee nominated by the Conference, the controlling majority had its plans laid in advance. To forestall the expected adverse report which the Committee would make to the General Conference, the board set up its own investigating committee. Its three members, all well known for their opposition to having the seminary on campus, made what Dean McClain called "perfunctory inquiries" of several teachers. Their attitudes, he wrote later, "made it clear that they had already decided that the college administration was right." Both L. S. Bauman and Rev. Charles H. Ashman came to the board meeting as members designated by the Southern California District, but under the new constitutional provision adopted by the college board in defiance of the General Conference disapproval, both men were refused a seat on the board. The minority who stood for the Statement of Faith fought valiantly but vainly. It had already become clear, from published statements of the college administration and its supporters, that they had fixed upon one of two alternate goals: they intended either to gain control over the General Conference of the denomination; or, failing this, they would move to take the college entirely out of the denominational control. The college attorney had already prepared a brief to show that the Brethren Church could not legally control the institution.

As Dean McClain got up to read his annual report to the board he anticipated to some extent the objective of the gathered men. Desiring to establish a historical record of the situation, he reviewed the events which led to the founding of the seminary at Ashland in 1930. He re-read some of the documents he had presented before the board in 1930, and called attention especially to Point 5 in the "Seminary Program" adopted that year by the board. It read:

> The continuance of the seminary on the college grounds should be regarded as an experiment for the present, and if it proves successful, steps shall be taken to erect a separate building suited to the special needs of the seminary. On the other hand, if the separation of the two institutions should be finally deemed advisable, both college and seminary shall cooperate in the matter so that it may be accomplished without injury to either.

The seminary dean then added: "Recent disappointments and difficulties might be discussed here at length from the seminary's standpoint, but I have no inclination to do so, unless such a course becomes necessary. It will be enough to say that my arguments for a separate location and autonomy for the seminary, uttered before this board seven years ago, are all valid today."

Professor McClain then recommended that the seminary be separated from the arts college. The report and recommendation were received in complete silence and filed with the secretary of the board.

Professor Hoyt, who had delivered the valedictorian address upon his graduation from Ashland College three years earlier, had been chosen from the ranks because of his brilliant record in seminary studies to teach Greek as a replacement for Dr. Ken Monroe who resigned. Now he was asked to appear before an investigating committee.

"It was not an investigation," Dr. Hoyt says now, looking back on the experience. "They had their minds made up. I was young . . . had no reputation. They were only going through the motions of an investigation."

As he came before the committee one of the members said: "Mr Hoyt, we want you to be truthful and honest in answering our questions."

"I assure you that I will be," he replied.

One of the questions was: "We know what students are saying but we don't think student testimony is any good."

"Well now," Professor Hoyt began, "I want to answer that. I was a student in this college for four years and became valedictorian. After I had gone through the college, you men felt that I was qualified to be a teacher in the seminary. Now, you are going to listen to the testimony of a student. If you don't like what I'm going to say then it comes right back on your heads because you men thought I was qualified to be a teacher."

At the close of the investigation, a member of the committee said, "Mr. Hoyt, I hope that you feel satisfied with this investigation."

"You asked me to be honest," Professor Hoyt replied, "so I'm going to be. I am not satisfied at all. You argued with every testimony presented, which shows that you men had your mind made up already."

"We never had a man talk to us like this," the committee replied.

"Well, you're getting one right now!" Professor Hoyt shot back.

The accused knew what was going to happen, but he said, "I took a stand right there. I knew they would let me go, but I had no idea they would let McClain go, too."

There was no record of Alva J. McClain's response to this investigating committee. Friends say he burned most of the unfortunate exchanges at Ashland out of courtesy to those who did the accusing and to those who were accused. The third was Melvin Stuckey who was retained in that brouhaha but fired two years later.

The letters of dismissal stopped short of making any specific charge of any kind toward any of the individuals examined. A published version referred vaguely to a lack of harmony between college and seminary, but made no attempt to explain what the problems were or who was responsible.

"Basically, there was only one problem," Professor McClain stated in his report, "and that was the problem of Christian Faith, and it was nothing new at Ashland College. The old problem had simply been dramatized by the broken promises of an administration which had publicly pledged itself to 'stand by' the school's own Statement of Faith. And the drama was heightened somewhat by the summary dismissal of two men who thought that promises should be kept."

In anticipation of what Professor McClain called

"widespread indignation" among the churches, the college published its Statement of Faith both in its current catalog and in a special bulletin sent out to the churches. It was dropped the following year and replaced by a "watered-down version of religion which left more room for 'liberal' and Unitarian variations." Professor McClain continued: "The publication of the Statement of Faith, of course, changed nothing. The real issue was not merely its publication, but rather its *application*. Upon this issue the college administration and faculty, by a roll-call vote, had already overwhelmingly rejected it."

The North Central Association smiled upon the change. "A division of the faculty," said the accrediting examiners, had now been remedied by certain "change" in personnel. Furthermore, "The new members on the staff appear to be merging their interests with those of Ashland College."

The implications of the report, to Professor McClain were unmistakeable and significant:

> In any conflict within a school over the restriction of "academic freedom" by the application of definite standards of Christian faith, almost any informed person knows to which side the average secular accrediting agency would lend its approval and support, especially if it knew that practically the entire staff was against the restriction.

From the seven lean years, Professor McClain drew a useful lesson: It is not enough to *have* a statement of faith. It is also necessary to bind the statement legally into the institution, and then have men with the will to support it.

Alva J. McClain

Father, Walter Scott McClain

The Aurelia, Iowa, farm house in which Alva J. McClain was born on April 11, 1888.

The McClain children, except for Arthur who died at the age of four;
Baby Fern Esther in the center, then clockwise beginning at seven o'clock:
Ruth Angeline, Alva J., Georgia Ada, Leslie Daniel, and Mary Ellen.

Arthur, Georgia, and Alva McClain in 1894, Aurelia, Iowa.

The McClain family during -year sojourn the Arizona Territory, 8-1900. From Left: Alva J., Mary Ellen, Mother Mary len, Georgia Ada, Ruth eline, Father Walter Scott McClain and .eslie Daniel.

The McClain family circa World War I, 1918: Back row from left: Georgia Ada, Mary Ellen, Leslie Daniel, Alva J., and Fern Esther. Front: Walter Scott, Ruth Angeline, and Mary Ellen.

Alva J. McClain

Josephine Gingrich McClain

The Sunnyside,
Washington,
Brethren Church
where Alva
McClain found
the Lord.

A busy day in Sunnyside

Alva and Josephine

Fishing in Bumping Lake, Washington helped Alva overcome stomach problems during seminary days at Xenia, Ohio.

Jo and Alva in
Long Beach.

Alva J. McClain relaxing at Long
Beach in 1922.

Alva J. McClain on the U.S.-Mexico
border at Tijuana, 1922.

Professor Alva J. McClain

Dr. Alva J. McClain at dedication of McClain Hall, the first building on the Winona Lake Grace Seminary campus.

Always dapper in dress, Professor McClain stands outside his Ashland, Ohio, house.

The house in Ashland, Ohio, where Alva and Jo lived when involved in Ashland Theological Seminary.

Alva J. McClain
with (from left):
Sister Mary
Ellen, wife
Josephine, and
sister Ruth.

Having fun on an outing in Palm Springs, California. From left:
Sister Ruth Angeline, wife Josephine, and sister Mary Ellen.

Alva and Jo in Winona Lake during earliest days of Grace Theological Seminary.

Dr. and Mrs. McClain with their Airstream trailer.

Dr. Alva J. McClain (far left) at the Scofield Bible Revision Committee banquet where the new Scofield Bible was introduced.

7

*A perspective on the drama
of Ashland's scissure*

Student Diary

The Rev. William H. Schaffer, a Brethren pastor for nearly 60 years (now retired), is a graduate of Ashland College's biblical studies program. His recollection of the campus maneuverings are still vivid in his memory, as recorded here especially for Dr. McClain's biography.

My first acquaintance with Alva J. McClain was when he came to Ashland College in 1925 to take over the Department of Theology. There was no seminary in those days. Theology was taught by J. Allen Miller and John H. Garber. Dr. Miller taught Greek; Dr. Garber taught homiletics. That was our theology, until Alva McClain came to start a systematic study. We soon discovered that the theology we had been taught was not strictly orthodox. It was laced with universalism and post millennialism, so we had to unlearn what we were taught the first two years and learn our theology over again.

During football season of 1926 our coach died. Nobody on the faculty had any experience with the game except Dr. McClain. He had played in high school and for the University of Washington, so the Ashland team got the school's theology professor out on the field where he finished the coach's term with some pretty fair instruction.

One autumn day I grabbed my shotgun and went out hunting to get the McClains a present. I brought back a ring-neck and gave it to the McClains. Later I was reprimanded by the authorities because hunters could shoot pheasants only every *other* day. I had shot on the wrong day, so they said, but there was no evidence. The McClains had eaten it.

After getting straightened out on my theology I was called to a pastorate in Hamlin, Kansas. I had first to be examined, so on July 1, 1927, I went before the Pennsylvania district. The full contingent couldn't come so Pastor Charles H. Ashman of Johnstown was to examine me. He asked me only one question: "Have you had any theology under Alva J. McClain?"

"Yes," I said, "I've had two years."

"That's enough for me," Pastor Ashman said. "I'll sign the ordination papers."

In 1936, Professor Melvin A. Stuckey went out to the California district with news about the problems in Ashland between the college and seminary administrations. The District chairman wrote to Dr. Anspach and asked him to explain what had happened to all of his promises. He didn't reply.

The district's appointed committee found that it wasn't going to be easy to carry out its mission. First of all, it was reduced to five members because of the resignation of R. D. Barnard and Roy Patterson with justifiable reasons. Then, after we drew up the questions we wanted to ask and the points we wanted to cover, George Ronk, the board chairman, told us we couldn't meet with the college administration until we had an invitation from them. So it was evident from the start that the will of the church had to conform to the will of the college, and not the other way around.

So, we did nothing until June 1, 1937, when the board met. I found out they were going to meet in the old Founders Hall so I slipped into the back with pad and pencil and took down everything.

The board in that session adopted a new constitution which included an amendment allowing an enlarged non-Brethren representation on the board. This weakened the church's control of the college. This was done by a vote of twenty-four to three, despite the vote of the 1936 conference against it.

The meeting of the trustees also considered dismissing McClain and Hoyt. The charges were that McClain and Hoyt had become *persona non grata* on campus, although they stopped short of saying that. When it came time to vote, Charlie Mayes called for a roll-call vote which the chairman quickly carried out. Each trustee voted orally and stated why he was voting as he did. Professor Garber said the seminary was costing too much money; Dr. W. S. Bell, the endowment secretary who had pushed so hard to get the seminary to Ashland, said that before the college had organized the seminary they were graduating men just as capable as any who graduated from the seminary in its original form. He cited as an example Pastor Herman Koontz then in Roanoke, Dr. R. D. Barnard then in Dayton, and a couple of others. He didn't mention me!

The only ones who voted not to dismiss McClain and Hoyt that day were Charles Mayes, editor of *The Brethren Evangelist,* and Dr. H. V. Wall, a physician from Long Beach, California.

Charles Mayes asked the question at the close of the meeting, "Now, what about the seminary?"

"There won't be any more seminary," the chairman stated. The majority agreed.

How to put together my report authorized by the Long Beach conference was the next question. I decided to ask Charlie Mayes. He suggested I write to as many students as I could get the names and addresses of and ask them what they had been taught at Ashland College during their four years there. So, I drew up a questionnaire and sent out fifty. Fifty replies came back, all expressing the conflict between college and seminary administrations during the last few years leading up to the break in 1937. So, I wrote my report and took it to the district.

The General Conference that year, 1937, met on August 23 in an atmosphere of tension. On Thursday morning, August 25, at a point of unfinished business I read my report of the investigating committee. It fully sustained the attitude of the seminary professors who had been dismissed. In case anybody wants to know what I said, here it is:

REPORT OF THE NATIONAL CONFERENCE
COMMITTEE ON THE INVESTIGATION OF
ASHLAND COLLEGE

We, your committee for investigating Ashland College, beg leave to submit to this conference the following report. Our duty as outlined by the last conference was "to thoroughly investigate the condition which is causing the disturbance at this conference."

Your committee organized and outlined a program of procedure before leaving the conference grounds. The president of this committee was authorized to contact the administration of Ashland College for the purpose of explaining more thoroughly the objectives of this committee and to ask for sympathetic cooperation. The president of our committee was informed, "I do not know when you expected to visit the institution inasmuch as the Board of Trustees must extend this invitation. Since the Board does not meet until March or April, I presume it will be necessary for your committee to delay its visit until after that date. The Board should discuss the matter fully and completely and then notify you as to its actions." Consequently the Committee did not actively function until the meeting of the Board of Trustees on June 1, 1937.

The minutes of this committee called for its next meeting at Ashland College at the time of the Board meeting. The secretary informed all members of this committee several weeks in advance, reminding them of the Ashland meeting. In the meantime, two members of this committee tendered their resignations. Two other members replied they could not come. One answered he would come on short notice if needed. The secretary of this committee also notified the President of the Board of Trustees and the President of the College of this committee's meeting at the same time of the College Board. After the organization of the Board of Trustees was affected the secretary of this committee was invited to attend the Board of Trustees sessions. One member of this committee, a member of the Board also, and the secretary, were present every minute of the Board sessions following the organization of the Board.

It being generally agreed that the "open letter" from the Southern California Brethren Ministerial Association caused much of the disturbance at last General Conference relative to Ashland College, the committee considered it their duty to investigate the protests made in that "open letter."

They are as follows:

1. That the adoption of the proposed amendment of the constitution would wrest the control of Ashland College from the Brethren Church. A vote against the adoption of this proposed amendment was registered at last general conference. The Board of Trustees of Ashland College in the last regular session in Ashland, June 1, 1937, adopted a new constitution including this amendment with a 24 to 3 vote.

2. It was also stated that there was growing antagonism between the Arts College and the Seminary. That the scriptural standards for the

"separated life" were not only held in derision but openly opposed by members of the Arts College faculty. This we found sustained in replies to a questionnaire mailed to a number of students and former students of the Brethren Church who attended Ashland College during the past seven years. This questionnaire was mailed June 22, 1937. The question read, "Is the atmosphere at Ashland College favorable towards the ministry and the spiritual Christian life?" With but one exception, the returned questionnaires declared that from the student's experience Ashland College did not strengthen their faith in Christ or the faith of any one else of their acquaintance but only as they came in contact with the Gospel Teams or Seminary activities. It was further stated that the general atmosphere at Ashland College towards the ministry and the spiritual Christian life was negative. Several instances were cited where young men came to Ashland with the intention of entering the ministry but declared that they lost that desire while yet in the Arts College and persuasion was against further study for the ministry and encouragement given to enter a more remunerative occupation.

3. It was also stated that members of the Arts College faculty openly questioned the statements of the Bible and others were utterly indifferent towards the great doctrines of the Bible. Our questionnaire brought to us this information under the question, "If you have known any professor antagonistic to 'the Faith . . .' state his or her viewpoint and what was said. Exact quotation not needed but the impression you received. Name the professor." Two professors openly denied the Virgin Birth of Jesus Christ. One professor openly ridiculed the Doctrine of the Blood Atonement. One professor upheld the scriptures one day and denied them the next but on the whole was not sympathetic to the Christian ministry and denied many of the Biblical statements dealing with origins. One professor worships at the throne of modernism. Several professors believe in salvation by good works of the "golden rule." One professor denied the New

Birth. One professor mocks the Second Coming of our Lord and prophecy in general. One professor doubts life after death and the resurrection body of the believer. One professor continually encourages students to attend the movies. One professor outlawed the carrying of a Bible into the classroom. One professor objected to citations from the Bible in a class room. One professor when upon an urgent demand of a class to state his position of faith did so in such a manner that it might be accepted by most any religionist. Only one professor in the Arts College was named as being an ideal professor in a Christian College and who, when opportunity afforded, clearly gave his testimony for his faith in the Holy Scriptures. It has been stated that student testimony is unreliable. We, however, are of the opinion that the most important thing between a teacher and a pupil is the impression the teacher leaves upon that pupil. If the teacher declares he or she has been misrepresented in these statements, how does he account for the fact that all these statements are signed by men and women who either directly or indirectly heard them. The majority of these men and women are willing to allow their names to be made public and some offer to make personal testimony to the facts of these statements. We further contend that a good professor always leaves a clear impression of what he or she wants the student to know.

4. It was also stated that the official weekly college publication known as the Ashland Collegian printed highly objectionable matter for a Christian institution. Not only did we find this to be true but the whole tenor of the paper was antagonistic to the principles of the nobler Christian life.

5. It was further stated that there was friction between the administration of Ashland College and the Ashland College Theological Seminary. This we found to be true. The Seminary faculty contended for strict adherence to the standards of faith and institutional objectives as printed in the College Catalog. It further contended that since Ashland College advertised itself as a Christian Institution the principles of the Christian faith should not be com-

promised. This condition led to an irreconcilable situation and culminated in the request for resignation or dismissal by the Board of Trustees of Alva J. McClain and Herman A. Hoyt of the Seminary faculty in an effort to bring peace among the faculties.

Your committee submits this report with a degree of reluctance inasmuch as sentimental value runs high. We feel, however, that in the face of stern duty we must submit this report to you according to the evidence. Our prayer is that somehow the Lord will overrule in these matters of unorthodoxy to the Biblical standards of Christian faith and practice and that Ashland College may stand upon the hill as an ever burning beacon to the eternal truth of God's infallible Word and that the Lord Jesus Christ may be exalted to His rightful place as the Savior of mankind through the shed blood of His Cross; His present intercession for the saints of God and the glorious hope of His Second Coming. This is our sincere prayer.

Dated: August 25, 1937.
(Signed) W. H. Schaffer
          C. A. Stewart
          R. F. Porte
          Ed Wolf
          Dr. Henry V. Wall

My report was so astonishing that the delegates asked me to read it again. Delegates seemed to be thrown into confusion and sides were quickly drawn. George Ronk criticized me for making that report based on student reports. I said I was using a biblical principle by asking the students instead of the professors. That's what the Lord said: "Don't ask me what I taught, ask those who heard me."

There was an amazing side issue in all of this. My father, a trustee at Ashland for 25 years, was a 32nd Degree Mason. When he read Dr. McClain's sermon on Freemasonry my father was furious. He denounced McClain for that. However, eight or nine years before he passed away he demitted from the Masonic Lodge.

"The whole thing's a fraud," he told me.

It was my privilege to report this to Dr. McClain in later years. My father had told me also that President Anspach was a Mason. One day he gave an address at the Masonic Lodge in Ashland. The papers reported the next day: "President of Ashland College says Masonry is the greatest organization in all the world."

Every man he suggested for the Ashland College board of trustees was a Mason. Some of the pastors on that board were Masons. L. S. Bauman had been wise to it. He said during the time of the dismissal of McClain and Hoyt, "The Masonic Lodge is responsible for putting McClain and Hoyt out of the seminary." And he was right.

Melvin Stuckey had warned at the California meeting, "Schaffer, if you don't retract that report you're through in the Brethren Church."

Two days after this meeting I was back in my church in Conemaugh. Who should drive up but W. S. Bell. I didn't tell him what was happening among the conservatives, but I asked him, "Dr. Bell, what about Ashland Seminary."

"You were there," he said. "You heard what they said. There will be no more Ashland Seminary."

I asked another board member and got the same answer. But as soon as the board found out the conservatives were going to form a seminary they changed their tune. They said, "Oh, there will *always* be an Ashland Seminary."

Not many people have any idea what we went through when we came back from the 1937 conference. We didn't know if we had a congregation or not. We had to fight every inch of the way. In Conemaugh, Pennsylvania, I had a divided congregation. There were a lot of Ashland sympathizers there who had infiltrated. But I happened to have the facts and finally swung them over to the Grace fellowship. Today that church is still in the Grace fellowship. That fall I was elected moderator of the Pennsylvania District. I served for 25 years as a board member of Grace Theological Seminary and I thank God for the privilege.

8

Amazing Grace

Following the fateful June 1, board meeting of 1937, Alva J. McClain had to decide carefully the next course of action. Of the 538 delegates at the 1937 General Conference, 275 would vote to receive the report of the investigating committee and 263 would vote not receive it. That meant that the church was divided evenly, with a large conservative constituency ready to see change. In addition, most of the seminary student body wanted their seminary to continue in what they considered to be the traditional viewpoint of the Brethren Church.

The evening of June 2, 1937 was the date of a historic prayer meeting in the home of Dr. J. C. Beal in Ashland. Dr. Beal had been a liberal teacher on the college campus years earlier, but after serving as a pastor he had abandoned these views and become a stalwart teacher of the Word of God.

In his home that night were gathered some of the conservative minority from the college board, members of the foreign missionary board which had been meeting at the same time, a few nearby pastors, and also representative students from both college and seminary. Someone remembered that Dr. L. S. Bauman was at a hotel downtown and rushed off to fetch him. There was not much discussion but there was general agreement that some provision should be made for the perpetuation of the ideals and faith of the seminary which had been founded seven years earlier. The gathered Brethren also wanted to care for the students who were already saying they could never return to the Ashland campus.

Without a human leader, the Brethren went to their knees in prayer. When they rose, Dr. L. S. Bauman took out his pen, wrote a personal check, and said: "I want to give the first gift to the new school."

Someone suggested that a paper be circulated for the signatures of all present who desired to work and pray for such a school. All signed except Professor Melvin A. Stuckey. He said he wanted first to determine what his status was at the college. Professor Stuckey had been the most vociferous critic of the "liberalism" on campus during his seven years as a seminary professor. Because of his position he had become intensely disliked by the college administration. Nevertheless, despite his frequent urging of students to "stand for truth no matter what," Dr. Stuckey remained with the Anspach group.

"He made his peace with the administration," Dean McClain said, "but at a cost which shocked his former colleagues and students."

The new seminary which grew out of the prayer meeting that night was called "The Brethren Biblical Seminary Association." On July 28 and 29 in that summer of 1937 its officers met in Philadelphia where it was decided that the name of the school would be "Grace Theological Seminary," and that its temporary location would be in the Ellet Brethren Church, Akron, Ohio. The decision was a response to the cordial invitation of the church's officials and pastor -- Raymond E. Gingrich, the second graduate of the seminary at Ashland.

If investigation revealed insurmountable legal and educational restrictions in Akron the minutes provided that the seminary would then be located in Fort Wayne, Indiana. No such difficulties were encountered, so the Ellet Brethren Church of Akron was the home of the new seminary until permanent quarters could be found.

Alva J. McClain and Herman A. Hoyt were extended a call to serve as professors, the former to take the position of president. Homer A. Kent, Sr., then pastor of the First Brethren Church of Washington, D. C., was invited to become a part-time teacher, "his teaching load and hours to be determined in such a manner as not to interfere with his present relationship as pastor of the Brethren Church at Washington, D. C."

Other prospective teachers were contacted and financial gifts began to come in. Dr. H. V. Wall was the first treasurer; F. B. Miller, then in the printing business in Akron, donated $1,000 worth of publicity material.

An executive committee made arrangements for publicizing the new venture, for procuring a charter, and for appealing for funds to support the new school. The estimated cost to launch and operate during the first year was calculated to be about $8,000. The leaders decided to lay before the National Conference in August for its approval and acceptance the plan for the new seminary as outlined by the Biblical Seminary Association.

In his *History of the Brethren Church*, p. 155, Homer Kent provides the atmosphere of the times:

Grace Seminary became the most talked-about institution in the Brethren Church. It became the rally-ing point of those who for so long had sought without success a rectification of conditions on the Ashland College campus. It became the object of bitter hatred on the part of those who could see no ill at Ashland. From then on The Brethren Church was divided in-to two groups of definite designations, the Ashland College group and the Grace Seminary group. The situation was discussed pro and con in every church, in district conferences, in the church paper, and through the mail and was sure to be a vital issue in the General Conference of 1937. The situation had already been brought into the open at the 1936 con-ference in connection with the appointment of the Ashland College investigation committee.

Following the organization of the Brethren Biblical Seminary Association, the Ashland College group formed an opposing organization which was called the Brethren Loyalty Association, Inc. headquartering in Ashland. This agency stressed loyalty to Brethren in-stitutions (Ashland College in particular) as being fun-damental to true Brethrenism. It viewed Grace Seminary as an enemy institution dramatically op-posed to the loyalty it advocated. Dr. W. S. Bell, in an article entitled "Who Are the Disturbers of Peace in the Brethren Church," wrote:

> *Why This Grace Seminary?* It is an organization that is dividing the Church. Two seminaries in a small denomination like ours, whose instructors are at variance with each other *means two churches.*
>
> *Who Authorized This Seminary?* A disaffected group that would impose their will on the College Board. A hand-picked group who asked no counsel but of themselves.

Obviously, Dr. Bell and his associates held the Grace Seminary group totally responsible for the division within The Brethren Church. For this reason, the General Conference was packed and interest was keen. When Pastor William Schaffer stood up to read the report of the investigating committee sharp division arose. The vote of 275 to receive the report and 263 not to receive it gives evidence of the division, although the motion lost because George Ronk invoked the two-thirds rule. The vote made it clear, however, that the new seminary had behind it a formidable following.

Alva J. McClain put the report of the investigating committee into perspective by showing that the college board had defied the 1936 Conference action by enlarging the non-Brethren representation on the board. Second, he emphasized that the report found that there was a growing antagonism between college and seminary due to the college's attitude toward spiritual standards of life and conduct. Third, that certain members of the college faculty had "openly questioned statements of the Bible and others were utterly indifferent towards the great doctrines of the Bible." Doctrines questioned included the Virgin Birth, Blood Atonement, the New Birth, the Resurrection, and the Second Coming of Christ. Fourth, material was being published in the college paper that was highly objectionable. Fifth, that the basic cause of the friction between the college administration and the seminary had been the insistence of the seminary upon strict adherence to the standards of faith which had been adopted by the board in 1933.

The promoters of the new seminary which was to open in Akron that October announced that all were invited to a special rally in the Winona Lake Presbyterian Church. Everyone at the General Assembly was invited, although it had no connection with the Conference. Since it was spearheaded by the conservatives, the Ashland Group expressed no interest and had no desire to participate. The ousted professors, the executive committee of the new school, and interested friends gathered nearly 500 strong to sing, pray, and hear plans for the opening of Grace Theological Seminary. Enthusiasm was unbounded.

Pioneer missionary to Africa, Estella Myers, stepped

forward at this rally with a personal check for $1,000 -- the largest single cash contribution to that date. This was a token to the gathered friends of God's favor upon the new venture. It also stimulated other gifts for the school.

Dr. William E. Biederwolf, director of the Winona Lake Christian Assembly, was so impressed by the vigor of the new work that he invited Grace Seminary to make its home at Winona Lake -- an invitation that would be accepted two years later.

Grace Theological Seminary opened in Akron, Ohio, on October 4, 1937, with a student body of thirty-nine. All of the former students in Ashland Seminary but two joined the Grace group. The Akron church extended warm hospitality to the new school. Classes met in every available space in the church. Chapel services were conducted in the main auditorium. The very limited library (books loaned by the faculty) was columned in a narrow space behind the rostrum. What the school lacked in facilities it made up with faculty and student enthusiasm. This spirit of fellowship was sustained by the evangelical churches of Akron. Many opened their pulpits to faculty and students for preaching missions.

On April 8, 1938, the legal charter under the laws of Ohio was received. The seminary was thus able to proceed as a fully organized institution. On June 3 of that year the first class was graduated -- three men, each receiving the bachelor of divinity degree. The members were: Kenneth B. Ashman, former president of the Ashland Seminary student body; Robert Miller; and Russell Williams. Each went on to become successful pastors within the group now known as The Fellowship of Grace Brethren Churches.

Grace Theological Seminary has been controlled by a board of trustees composed of twenty-seven members of The Grace Brethren Church elected to serve for a period of three years each. Of course, there may be re-elections. The first permanent board was elected at the first corporation meeting held in the Presbyterian Church at Winona Lake, Indiana, on September 2, 1938. Prior to this, however, due to a requirement of the law, there had been a temporary board of trustees composed of the original members of the advisory council of the seminary association, exclusive of those who were mission pastors or salaried employees of national boards. This temporary board had served during the 1937-38 school year.

The ultimate control of the seminary rests in a body of corporate members composed of those who give to its financial support and are in agreement with its purposes. This corporation is responsible for the election of the members of the board of trustees. This type of organization is similar to that used by the Foreign Missionary Society of the Brethren Church, which has proved so successful in the operation of that organization since 1900. This type of organization, together with a carefully prepared statement of faith to which each trustee and teacher is required "to subscribe annually in writing" seems to have secured Grace Theological Seminary as a stronghold for orthodoxy.

For two years Grace grew in the confined facilities of the Ellet Church of Akron until it could no longer contain the burgeoning student body. After careful consideration of other places for a permanent location, the school moved to Winona Lake, Indiana, in response to Dr. Biederwolf's invitation, to begin its operation there in the fall of 1939. The school occupied the upper floor of the three-story national headquarters building of the Free Methodist Church. In a cordial atmosphere and a central location the school looked forward to prosperous days.

The disconnection of the two groups was not yet ready to be laid to resolved. Dr. McClain's spunky sister Ruth, who had attended most of the General Conferences, asked her former Sunnyside Pastor W. S. Bell, "Do you mean to tell me that everything that you have done in this conference has been fair and square?"

"Well," he replied, "under the circumstances, yes!"

Alva J. McClain wrote in *The History of Grace Theological Seminary* for the 1951 yearbook:

At the General Conference of 1939, the time that Grace Seminary moved to Winona Lake, a very large attendance of delegates was indicated. The membership committee, controlled by the Ashland group by the narrow margin of one vote, rejected a group of 81 credentials presented by delegates from churches supporting Grace Seminary. Apparently these credentials had been held back until the Ashland College group was fairly certain that they had a majority among the delegates already seated. Then the committee brought in a recommendation to reject the 81, and the majority of Ashland supporters was able to adopt the recommendation, thus guaranteeing that no future action could change their majority.

The charge against the 81 rejected delegates was that they had supported "competing organizations" (a primary reference to Grace Seminary). The hypocrisy of this charge was made clear by the fact that the committee had already seated the president of Grace Seminary as well as most of its board of trustees! But they had waited with their unfair maneuver until they had a very large block of credentials before revealing their scheme.

Somewhat appalled by the brazen character of these tactics, and convinced that the entire action was an illegal violation of the Conference rules, the supporters of Grace Seminary (now held to a fixed minority) refused to vote upon any motion throughout the Conference. Other delegates, noting the situation, did not even bother to present their credentials.

It was this totally unexpected and palpably illegal violation of its own rules that delivered the General Conference into the hands of the Ashland party. The sole recourse left to the injured delegates was an appeal to the civil courts, which was precluded for them by the Biblical precept against the initiation of such action, long held by the Brethren. The injured churches did the only thing possible for them under the circumstances, in declaring the entire General Conference to be un-Brethren and without any ecclesiastical authority. These churches and their pastors, comprising about one half of the denomination at the time, returned the next year to hold the General Conference at Winona Lake under its original and time-honored rules. The Ashland group took their general conference to Ashland College, at Ashland, Ohio. Thus the division of Brethren congregations into two conferences was brought about.

The issue of congregational government in the Brethren Church was finally determined in the Ohio courts, where an Ashland College minority in the First Brethren Church of Dayton sued the large majority and pastor for possession of the property. The argument of the minority was that the majority had become non-Brethren because they refused to support Ashland College and the general conference which it controlled. In both the lower and highest Ohio courts, it was decided that the Brethren Church was truly "congregational" in government and therefore no local church could be bound by any ecclesiastical organization outside itself. Any Brethren congregation was free to support or not support any conference or educational institution.

But there were miles to go before the two would once again consociate in Christian fellowship many years later.

9

A Gentle Reign

Alva J. McClain was 51 at the start of the golden years in Winona Lake. He and Jo settled into a rented house at 4th and College, four blocks from the Free Methodist headquarters on College Avenue where the new school met. Later they built around the corner at 5th and Walnut a house which the professor himself designed. Grace Seminary was a tightly knit team in those days: President McClain, who drew enrollees on the strength of his reputation . . . Dean Herman Hoyt, the architect of the curriculum and business manager . . . Mrs. McClain, bookkeeper and financial secretary.

Dr. McClain had brought certain changes to Brethren thinking. His theological system was spearheaded by an emphasis on God's grace. He emphasized the believer's assurance of salvation, the believer's security, the pre-millennial, personal return of Christ for His Church, and outlines on the brilliant arguments of the Apostle Paul in *The Epistle of Paul to the Romans* on law and grace.

His classrooms were relaxed and informal, yet students offered the little Scot undivided attention. Some things he taught were not always easy to grasp the first time out. One budding preacher, listening to his professor's explanation of God's sovereignty, raised his hand and was acknowledged: "Dr. McClain, since God knows what is going to happen ahead of time then he knows whether or not I'm going to pass my theology exam, so why should I study?"

"Young man," Dr. McClain exclaimed, his forefinger waving, "if you don't study for this exam you are predestined to fail!"

Proud new fathers liked to pass around the candy box to announce the birth of sons and daughters. Dr. McClain consistently expressed a love for children, although he and Jo had none of their own, but he always had a word of caution for the men he thought should be giving priority to education: "There is no one in this school named Noah," he reminded.

In the middle of a class one unfortunate student who had probably worked the night shift at the local foundry to keep bread on the table, fell asleep. A "friend" next to him jabbed him and whispered, "Pssst. Dr. McClain just called on you to pray."

The bleary-eyed student jumped to his feet, prayed for God's blessing upon the class, and sat down. Dr. McClain looked up, surprised. "Now that our brother is finished with his prayer," he said, "we'll go on with the class."

Still others had to be gently corrected when they prayed phrases like, "Still our beating hearts . . ." and "bless us as we break the Word . . . ." All the same, the professor emphasized that one should not determine a person's theology by the passions of his prayers.

One day when Dr. Hoyt was writing on the blackboard questions for an examination the class grew quiet in worried anticipation. Right in the middle of the tenseness Bob Hill sang out: "Have you tried Wheaties?"

On another occasion, Dr. McClain suggested that the class sing a hymn to begin the period. Bob stood up and belted out: "I was under the spout when the blessings came out, Hallelujah! I'm foursquare now."

Said Dr. McClain, unamused, "Let us pray."

A canary named "Phibby" was the subject of many an illustration in the classroom. It's not known exactly how it happened, but his pet canary somehow broke its leg. Dr. McClain repaired it successfully and nurtured that bird devotedly until demise. Phibby's name was a shortened version of "Mephibosheth" [see II Samuel 4:4], the lame son of Jonathan whose nurse dropped him when she "made haste to flee." Dr. McClain told his class that he saw no biblical reason why he might not see his bird some day in heaven.

In the golden days of Winona Lake, illness continued to interrupt. Mrs. McClain looked after her husband devotedly, kept tidy their modestly furnished house, and ran interference if too many students came calling when her husband was not feeling well. Some went in pairs: one to engage Mrs. McClain in conversation while the other slipped in to see their professor. She had the patience of Job and the kind of even temperament that enhanced their ordered lives that confessed the beauty of God's grace. Jo needed that patience, for her husband was a perfectionist, albeit a patient perfectionist. He once read an entire book by Albert Schweitzer in order to write one paragraph in his volume, *The Greatness of the Kingdom*.

Dr. McClain corrected anyone who might call him "Scotch," explaining that he was "Scottish." He was particularly fond of plaid designs. According to Mary Hammers, McClain plaids are still available in Scotland.

Mary remembers how patiently Professor McClain worked with her on the Ashland campus when the seminary relocated its library. She had had no experience cataloguing books but Dr. McClain, "a perfectionist, yes, but the kindest perfectionist I ever knew," helped her get each volume correctly placed and identified on the shelves.

He embraced moderately the Calvinist TULIP (Total depravity, Unconditional election, Limited atonement, Irresistible grace, and the Perseverance of the saints) but did not believe in eternal security at the expense of holy living. He called for a balance between divine sovereignty and human responsibility. He embraced a balanced dispensationalist view of the Bible, but believed a difference had to be made between Israel and the Church.

In 1951 when the seminary moved with 194 students into McClain Hall built on seven acres east of town, illness was holding Dr. McClain to half a teaching load. Five major setbacks had weakened his body. First came the serious baseball spiking in 1910 which ended his ball-playing career. An appendectomy was performed while he was a student in college. In 1935 surgeons removed a foot of ulcerated colon which resulted in a colostomy (later corrected). He didn't mind talking about his operation but when Ben Hamilton came up to a cluster of students listening to the professor describe the procedure he didn't make himself popular with the remark, "I guess that makes you a semi-colon."

For a year, Dr. McClain suffered what his sisters termed a nervous breakdown. Dr. McClain described his ailment as "vertigo." When he lifted his head off the pillow he said the world turned upside down.

"I'd rather have a weak body and be humble before the Lord," he once said.

At his right hand was Herman Hoyt, the man from Dallas Center, Iowa, whose boyhood ambition was to play football. That changed when he got to Ashland

College in 1928. After a successful season he told his coach, "I came to college to get something," and he got it. He took the top grades at Ashland, delivered the valedictorian address, and was selected by the faculty to teach Greek and Hebrew.

"I first heard Dr. McClain speak in the Ashland First Brethren Church when I enrolled in the college and I'll be frank," said Dr. Hoyt, "I never heard a sermon like that in my life. He impressed me by his handling of the text, which was II Corinthians 3:18. I said to myself, 'I hope I can preach like that some day.' I never dreamed at that time that I would sit under his ministry and then be with him on the college faculty and later in the founding of Grace Seminary. Dr. McClain could teach the whole counsel of God; he could also take something that wasn't worth a piffle and make you think it was the greatest thing in the world."

It became apparent in the late forties that the National Fellowship of Brethren Churches had no place to send students from its churches except to Grace Theological Seminary, a graduate school. The establishment of a college, therefore, was forced upon them. With the addition of the collegiate division, the student body increased in 1948 by 32 students, by 45 in 1949, and by 50 in 1950, making the total registration for those years 117, 144, 194.

Dr. McClain felt a keen loyalty to established local churches when the seminary moved to Winona Lake. For many years he resisted the starting of a Brethren church in the community, believing that such a congregation would not be greeted warmly by the established churches. So it was with consternation that he heard about a group of seminarians who were organizing a church in nearby Warsaw under sponsorship of the General Association of Regular Baptists. There was already a Baptist church in Warsaw, pastored by William Sweeting. In a letter to John Stoll, Dr. McClain said in part:

. . . We did not want anyone to feel that we were in any way bringing pressure on anybody because we value the freedom which we have in this country. I told the young men that of course they had a perfect right to start a church if they so desired. However, I did feel somewhat regretful that in the launching of this group some students at Grace Seminary were involved . . . .

Dr. McClain often said in his classes, "It's too bad that just when a man gets to the place where he knows a few things he grows weak and then dies." Precisely because this is true, the board constantly urged him to put into books his accumulated knowledge. But when a person is not feeling well, any writing project can be overwhelming. On one occasion when he took his trailer into Yellowstone National Park for some vacation fishing and for time to write, Dr. McClain spent an entire afternoon forming one sentence.

In 1959 he saw finally the publication of his most significant work, *The Greatness of the Kingdom*. It was published first by the Zondervan Publishing House and presented as Volume 5, to be one of six major reference books by Alva J. McClain. However, "Volume 5" turned out to be his only major work. In 1968 Moody Press picked up the book and in 1974 BMH Books published the third printing.

Aside from his writing, Dr. McClain served as a member of the revision committee for *The New Scofield Reference Bible* (1954-1963). He was a charter member of the Evangelical Theological Society and later a member of the American Scientific Affiliation.

As his strength declined, he turned over more and more of his duties to the men whom he affectionately called his "brethren." They took from his heart the burden of business cares and administration, they filled pulpits for him, assisted in editing his writings, and graded his papers. Herman A. Hoyt became president of Grace Schools in 1962, Homer A. Kent, Jr., in 1976 and John J. Davis in 1986.

"Mick" sat and watched with patriarchal calm the deliberations of the school he had led so brilliantly for a quarter of a century. Students had to get used to seeing other men at his desk . . . congregations had to invite others to their pulpits . . . publishers were resigned never to having those other big volumes which were to have been written by the man from Grace.

In 1962 he officially retired from teaching. Parkinson's Disease had crept in and old age added its final insult. On November 11, 1968, at the age of eighty years, a few months after Dr. Hoyt had driven him and Mrs. McClain to Waterloo, Iowa, where they moved into Friendship Village Retirement Home, he passed into the presence of his Lord. His body was transported by automobile back to Winona Lake for burial in Warsaw, Indiana, near his school.

And so his body rests now among the tall old trees that nod and sway. The tramp of feet as students make their way to class no longer reaches his ears but their cheerful shouts would still be music, could he but hear them. He understands perfectly now the Grace of God that passes understanding upon earth and would say even more strongly today. "Well, of course, *I* believe . . ."

And now, so do we all.

10

*His final chapel message
in May, 1962*

Lest We Forget

Twenty-five years ago, when I was called to the presidency of this school, it became my privilege to formulate the central purpose embodied in our charter: "To know Christ and to make Him known as the only Savior and Lord of life."

Now the time has come for me to address you at this final chapel service as your president. And I feel that I can do nothing better than to point your eyes and minds once more to Him who is "able to keep you from falling and to present you faultless before the presence of his glory with exceeding joy."

My text is brief, the first three words of II Timothy 2:8 in the American Standard Version -- "Remember Jesus Christ." You may forget me, what I have said, and what I have done. I shall not complain. I ask of you but one thing: that you will always "remember Jesus Christ."

A dear friend of mine used to say concerning the Lord Jesus Christ, "He never could have done what He did if He had not been who He was!" Who *was* Jesus? Upon this question hang vast and eternal issues. The entire plan of salvation, the whole structure of gospel truth, the total content of divine revelation -- yes, all our hopes for time and eternity rest upon the answer to this question.

And God has answered this question. For all divine revelation speaks with one voice about the matter. Six hundred years before the birth of our Lord, Isaiah saw his glory and named Him "Wonderful, Counselor, The Mighty God, the Everlasting Father, the Prince of Peace." Micah spoke of Him as the one "whose goings forth are of old, from everlasting." And John, that disciple whom Jesus loved, wrote of Him as the "Eternal Word" -- "God manifest in the flesh." This is the answer -- God's answer -- to the question, "Who is Jesus?" He was and is the infinite and eternal God.

There is little danger that the world will ever forget that there was once on earth a person named Jesus of Nazareth. All the unbelief and skepticism of man could never efface wholly the imprint of His footsteps in human history. But there is real danger that the world, and even the professing church, may forget who Jesus is! And I think that the devil would be wholly content to have us remember the *man* Jesus and forget who He is. Therefore, it is my business, it is your business, and the business of this school, to make sure that in our presence no one shall ever forget that Jesus is *"the Lord . . ." Kurios . . . -- Jehovah . . . the great "I Am."*

There is great blessing and power in knowing who Jesus is. Remember who He is, and you will never be ashamed to confess Him before men. Remember who He is and you will never have any doubts about your eternal salvation.

John wrote of Him, "The Word became flesh." And Paul pointed the Corinthian church to "the grace of our Lord Jesus Christ, who, though he was rich, yet for your sakes he became poor." Again, writing to the Philippians, he exhorted them to have the mind of Christ, who, "existing in the form of God . . . emptied himself, taking the form of a servant, becoming in the likeness of men." The eternal Son of God became flesh, became poor, became a servant, became in men's likeness.

Who can measure the infinite distance of His descent? When we have reached the limits of our human comprehension, we can only say in wonder and awe, "The Eternal God has become man," and fall upon our faces and worship.

Let us remember what He became. If we remember how He stooped from heaven to earth, it will help us to stoop. If we remember how He "humbled himself," it will help us to humble ourselves. For it is not easy for us to bend. In fact, the natural man will never bend to the will of God. We are often proud, hard, and unyielding. We bend to the will of God only as this incarnate Lord of ours dwells fully within us and the spirit of His condescension becomes our spirit.

Here, lest I might be misunderstood, I hasten to add that when our Lord "become man," though His humanity was real, just as real as yours or mine, yet He did not give up His divine personality. To put the matter in other words, "when He became what He did, He did not cease for an instant to be who He was." For that would have been impossible. As to His divine person He is always "Jesus Christ the same yesterday, and today, and forever."

The Scriptures explain that "he died for our sins." "He was wounded for our transgressions." "He loosed us from our sins in his own blood." What does all this mean? It means that God in Christ went to Calvary and there put His own person in the stead of us who are sinners; that He bore in His own body all the terrible recompense that we deserved; that He paid in full all the debt and demerit of human sin; that by the Cross He established an infinite credit, as it were, upon which we as sinners may now draw for pardon and righteousness and life.

But words are weak and language fails when we try to speak of what Christ did when He died for men. You must come to Calvary for yourself and there experience for yourself all the blessedness of pardon unlimited and the life eternal.

Let us remember what Christ did when He died: in our songs, in our worship, in our thanksgiving, in our fellowship at the table of the Lord: but above all, let us remember what He did by what we do for Him. This is the way that God remembers us. Three times in the Book of Genesis we read that "God remembered" someone. And each time there follows a record of something that God did for the one remembered.

I shall always be deeply concerned about the missionary vision and consecration of this school. I am expecting even greater here in future days in the way of missionary activity than in the past. And I know that I shall not be disappointed if you -- both faculty and students -- will only remember what Christ did for you when he died and rose again. There is no other missionary motive so filled with power.

Frances Havergal was not wrong when she placed on the lips of our Lord the words of her great hymn, "I gave, I gave My life for thee; what hast thou given for Me?"

There is a false cult with us today which claims that Christ came back from heaven in 1874 and is now on earth setting up His kingdom. And in the professing church there are a few theologians who solemnly declare that Jesus never went away! All such ideas, of course, are a delusion. Our Lord in person is not on earth today. *He is in heaven.* This is an important certainty of Christian faith of which altogether too little is being preached.

The presence of Christ in heaven bears strong witness to at least four great Christian facts. It witnesses, first of all, to the perfect righteousness of the Son of God himself. Second, it declares that the awful penalty for our sins has been paid -- paid to the last farthing! Third, His presence in heaven guarantees that we, too, shall someday be there. A fourth fact which is not so well known is that our Lord entered heaven to sit upon a throne -- not upon the throne of His own kingdom, or upon a throne of judgment, but upon a throne of grace!

What does all this mean to us? It means for one thing that the only Being in the universe who has the right to sit in judgment upon sinners is now seated on a "throne of grace." Nothing like this has ever happened before. In all the ages of human history past, no age was ever like the one in which we live today. Grace -- the grace of God in Christ -- is on the throne!

On this throne there are inscribed some words, very precious words: "Let us therefore draw near unto the throne of grace, that we may receive mercy, and may find grace to help in time of need." With our little minds we might have supposed that the grace of God had been exhausted in the cross. But no! Here is more grace, present grace, grace to help us in time of need! To supply this present grace, our blessed Lord is in heaven. Let us not forget where He is.

Our Lord made many promises but there is one which I like to call "The Promise." "If I go," He said, "I will come again, and receive you unto myself; that where I am, there ye may be also."

These are days when we need to remember the promise of His coming. There seems to be on every hand a dearth of the "upward look." Even the professing church in some quarters has adopted a philosophy which is of the earth -- earthy! The evolutionists are preaching a "gospel of the dirt." They are teaching our young people to look downward, within themselves, for the world's deliverance. In such an hour, may God keep us looking upward for that final and complete redemption which is to come down from heaven with "the appearing of our great God and Savior, Jesus Christ." And this "upward look" will be the surest evidence that we have not forgotten Him.

I have asked you to remember who Christ was, what He became, what He did at Calvary, where He is, and what He promised. All this is good, but it's not good enough. You might remember all this and yet fall far short of "remembering" Jesus Christ. Therefore, in this final word, I charge you to remember the Lord Jesus Christ himself, and for himself. I am sure He is pleased when we love Him for what He has done for us. But I am also sure that He yearns to be loved for himself -- to be remembered for himself, just for himself.

In an advertisement of a popular memory system I once saw a huge picture of a man. And beneath the picture were these words: "The man with the million-dollar memory." It is not given to all of us to possess that kind of memory. (There have been times when I would have been content if my students had even a thousand-dollar memory.) Be that as it may, all of us can have a memory infinitely more precious in the sight of God -- a memory upon which there is stamped indelibly and forever the glorious image of the Son of God, our Lord and Savior.

> *"Lord God of Hosts, be with us yet,*
> *Lest we forget, lest we forget."*

Divine Appointments

Born
April 11, 1888, Aurelia, Iowa

Parents
Walter Scott and Mary Gnagey McClain

Married
June 7, 1911 to Josephine Gingrich, La Porte City, Iowa

Education
University of Washington, 1908-1909
The Bible Institute of Los Angeles, 1914-1915
Xenia Theological Seminary, Xenia, Ohio, Th.M. in 1925
Antioch College, Yellow Springs, Ohio, 1917
Occidental College, B.A. with highest honors, 1925

Honorary Degrees
D.D., The Bible Institute of Los Angeles, 1940
LL.D., Bob Jones University, Cleveland, Tennessee 1945

Ordination
To the Ministry of the Brethren Church

Pastorate
First Brethren Church, Philadelphia, Pa., 1918-1923

Teaching Positions
Professor of Apologetics, Philadelphia School of the Bible, 1919-1923
Professor of Theology, Ashland College and Seminary, Ashland, Ohio, 1925-1927
Professor of Christian Doctrine, Bible Institute of Los Angeles, 1927-1929
Professor of Theology and Apologetics, Ashland Theological Seminary, Graduate School of Ashland College, 1930-1937
President and Professor of Christian Theology and Apologetics, Grace Theological Seminary, 1937-1962

Other Positions
Educational Editor, *The Brethren Herald*, 1940-1962
Trustee and Candidate Secretary, Foreign Missionary Society of the Brethren Church, 1917-1967
Moderator, General Conference of Brethren Churches, 1930 and 1934
Member, Board of Directors, Winona Lake Christian Assembly, Inc., 1941-1962
Secretary, *ibid.*, 1947-1956
Member: Phi Beta Kappa National Honor Society
Member: National Association of Biblical Instructors
Member: Evangelical Theological Society
Member: The American Scientific Affiliation

Writings

Outline and Argument of St. Paul's Epistle to the Romans

The Doctrine of the Kenosis in Philippians

Christian Faith, Its Nature, Object, and Intelligible Medium

Current Tendencies Which Limit Christian Faith

Daniel's Prophecy of the 70 Weeks (translated into Portuguese)

The Jewish Problem and Divine Solution

The Greatness of the Kingdom

Bible Truths (translated into Sango for Africa)

Inspiration of the Bible

The "Problems" of Verbal Inspiration

Law and Grace

The Threefold Ministry of Christ and Three Appropriate Symbols

Romans, the Gospel of God's Grace, compiled from lectures, edited by Herman A. Hoyt, published posthumously in 1978.

Grace Schools Today

In the years since Dr. McClain's presidency Grace Schools have continued to develop. As the founder and first president McClain served from 1937 to 1962. He was succeeded by Dr. Herman A. Hoyt (1962-1976); Dr. Homer A. Kent, Jr. (1976-1986); and Dr. John J. Davis (1986 —   ).

Grace Theological Seminary has experienced steady growth from its early years, leveling off with an enrollment in excess of 400 during the 1980s. Degrees offered are the M.Div., Th.M., Th.D., M.A. in Biblical Counseling, M.A. in Christian School Administration, and M.A. in Missions. As sponsor of the International Institutes of Christian School Administrators and of Christian Teachers, Grace Seminary has an international reputation as a leader in the Christian School movement. The seminary received accreditation from the North Central Association of Colleges and Schools in 1982.

Grace College has likewise achieved substantial growth in enrollment, reaching a high of 931 in 1981. The college offers both B.A. and B.S. degrees with a variety of programs. In 1979 the first students were enrolled in an associate degree program in nursing. Grace's athletic teams are viewed as serious contenders in the Mid Central Conference. Choirs, instrumental groups, and dramatic productions have brought wide recognition to the college. Accreditation was granted to Grace College in 1976 by the North Central Association of Colleges and Schools.

Acquiring of additional land and construction of new facilities accompanied the growth of Grace Schools. Two dormitories, Alpha Hall (1964) and Beta Hall (1966) were built to accommodate college students. The Morgan Library was erected in 1969, the Cooley Science Center was completed in 1978, Colonial Hall was renovated to house the Art Department in 1981, and Alpha Dining Commons was expanded that same year. The Grace campus now encompasses 150 acres with assets totalling $12.8 million. The library houses more than 150,000 books and microforms. In 1968 Grace Schools assumed control of the property and facilities of the Winona Lake Christian Assembly, which operates the well-known Bible Conference grounds. Many of its facilities are utilized for the educational and residential needs of Grace Schools.

The vision of Dr. McClain and those around him has resulted in two schools that have provided education and leadership for young people and Christian enterprises that circle the globe. As Grace completes its first half-century and looks to the future, its foundation upon the Word of God is as firmly held as ever, and the need for its ministry is just as great. May God grant as bright a future as He has provided victory in the past.